MINIATURE GARDENS

THE GARDENER'S HANDBOOK: A SERIES OF USEFUL BOOKS—VOLUME 4
DR. JOHN PHILIP BAUMGARDT, GENERAL EDITOR

Joachim Carl

MINIATURE GARDENS

Translated from the Second Edition by
Martin Kral

TIMBER PRESS
Portland, Oregon

ISBN 0-88192-164-5
Printed in Hong Kong

TIMBER PRESS, INC.
9999 S.W. Wilshire
Portland, Oregon 97225

Library of Congress Cataloging-in-Publication Data

Carl, Joachim.
    [Miniaturgärten. English]
    Miniature gardens / Joachim Carl ; translated from the second
edition by Martin Kral.
        p.   cm. -- (The Gardener's handbook ; v. 4)
    Translation of: Miniaturgärten.
    Includes bibliographical references.
    ISBN 0-88192-164-5
    1. Gardens, Miniature.   I. Title.   II. Series: Gardener's
handbook (Portland, Or.) ; v. 4.
    SB433.5.C3713   1990
    712--dc20   89-20412
                                                              CIP

Contents

Preface

Human beings have always wanted to claim part of nature for themselves and to reproduce it in their own gardens. This book is intended to guide those who wish to recreate such a piece of nature with enduring, hardy plants—not merely with the showy spectacle of colorful flowers. Those gardeners interested in specific groups of plants will find the almost inexhaustible variety of alpine and mountain plants a fascinating world, full of delightful experiences. Further, it is possible to nurture and grow such plant treasures in even the smallest of spaces. One can usually find room in a garden corner for a miniature rock garden or a small bed of alpines, and there is always a place for a container on a patio. There is no better setting for the magical beauty of alpine plants than in these miniature gardens. Karl Foerster, the grand master of perennial plants, noted in his book *The Rock Garden of the Seven Seasons* that rock gardens are treasure-chests for the gems of the plant world. Herein I describe how to make such treasure-chests and how to plant them for satisfying, long-lasting displays.

One particular difficulty in a book aimed at both the layman and the specialist is the matter of botanical names. Common trade names do not always tally with the precise scientific names. So far as possible, common names and their synonyms have been retained in this book, and plant descriptions kept brief. Coombes' *Dictionary of Plant Names* (Timber Press, Portland, Oregon) is a useful reference to help sort out these nomenclatural difficulties.

A special "thank you" goes to Emil Wetter for his accurate illustrations. Mrs. Martel Hald also receives heartfelt thanks for her many words of advice.

Joachim Carl

Origin and Development of Hardy Miniature Gardens

Two great cultural streams have contributed to gardening as we know it today. On the one hand there is the formal gardening style developed in Europe, the Middle East and India; on the other the more natural, yet stylized garden design developed in China and Japan. In the West the rules of symmetry dominate, while the Far East tradition focuses upon a natural positioning of plants down to the smallest detail. Oriental gardening involves a juxtaposition of spirit and nature, exemplified by the interplay of rocks and plants. This is reflected in the East's art in which a few rocks or stones are combined with individual, often bizarre, plant formations, replicating nature in miniature. This gardening style was introduced into Europe (via Great Britain) in the 19th century. At the same time, a nearly inexhaustible supply of hardy perennials developed as a result of growing interest in mountain climbing and the subsequent cataloging of alpine plants. The British became eminent in this pursuit. Simultaneously with alpine sports, they began to collect plants from all over the Empire; we have to be particularly grateful that their preference for montane regions, notably the Alps and the mountains of the Himalayas, led to the introduction of ever more plants from these regions into our gardens.

Through the mingling of Asian design concepts and the greater acceptance of alpine flora, the art of the rock garden developed, perhaps nowhere more than in Great Britain. Consequently, British growers pioneered rockery design and the cultivation of alpine plants.

Rocks can play an important role in any garden. Frequently they are the principle element in a natural design, since with rocks and boulders one can create convincing displays in gardens of limited size.

The main objective of Far Eastern garden design derived from a religious, contemplative aspect, pushing imitation of natural surroundings to the fore but avoiding elaborate means except for a few, especially naturalistic rocks and one or several bizarre plant forms. English growers, by contrast, moved plants into the foreground, the design merely providing the frame for the plants themselves. A similar approach was taken by other European gardeners. There, the creation of rockeries and alpine gardens arose from the need to transplant and tend the flora found in nearby mountain regions. In the mid-19th century the first rock gardens developed in Alpine monasteries and in gardens adjoining the hunting estates of the nobility.

Space was not a requirement for such collections, since wildflowers and alpine plants are ideal for recreating entrancing vignettes of nature in small nooks. Soon, however, it became apparent that plants which were difficult to grow were more successfully cultivated in separate alpine gardens, since such collections themselves needed more care and attention.

In England the more diligent or dedicated collectors planted their treasures in clay pots and small containers. Since the cultivation of hardy plants required long-term care, efforts were made to find vessels that were thick, durable, and could withstand frost damage. At first, collections were displayed in stone mortars and so-called 'hand mills'. Soon, troughs hewn from rock and first made to water farm animals were pressed into service. Some of these were as small as 9 × 12 in. (20 × 25 cm), and were used to display only one plant variety.

In the early 1920s Clarence Elliot, a great admirer of alpine flora and owner of the rock garden nursery Six Hills used containers for display. Soon the first articles about container gardens appeared. In the British Isles these articles led to a widespread acceptance of container gardening. One reason for this was that container gardens proved to be a successful method of successfully cultivating otherwise difficult or sensitive plants. For example, very particular mixtures of soil could be prepared for use in such containers. Tiny or slow-growing tufts grew better in containers than in larger, more exposed rockeries or in an alpine garden. Further, a plant collection can be viewed in isolation in such vessels and at much greater proximity than is possible in a rock garden.

Container gardening, therefore, developed for reasons other than simply aesthetic. It proved to be a genuine means of successfully cultivating plants that were known to be difficult to raise out of the wild. Among English devotees of container gardening, this form of cultivation soon came to be known as the "most fascinating hobby in the world."

During the early 1930s, the first troughs filled with alpine flowers appeared in London's Chelsea Flower Show—provided by Clarence Elliot again, who paved the way for these miniature garden collections. He collected troughs hewn from soft limestone, mostly with the dimensions of 8 × 12 in. (20 × 30 cm), 12 × 20 in. (30 × 50 cm), and 2½ × 3 ft. (75 × 90 cm), which then were sold fully planted with alpine collections.

But soon the supply of these old English livestock watering troughs was exhausted. No matter. Old stone kitchen sinks would serve the same purpose, although most were only 4 in. deep. But these too came into short supply, so since lovers of container gardens also happen to be very individualistic, a new form of container was devised and given the name "slab garden" by Mr. Simpson-Hayward, who was instrumental in encouraging their use. Instead of a trough he used a stone slab, supported by rocks. Irregularly-formed rocks were then cemented onto the slab, and the interstices filled with an appropriate growing medium. Into these crevices and niches he then planted diverse alpine plants. Calcareous tufa proved ideal for the creation of such slab gardens and provided a useful base even for otherwise difficult plants. Together with the sinks, these slab gardens became the predecessors of our contemporary alpine container gardens.

Only slowly was this method of displaying alpine plants in troughs and larger containers accepted by non-British growers. Some initial trials were made before World War II, but only in the post-war era did container gardening really begin to take off. In Austria, Dr. Rosenstingl of Gmunden became widely known for miniature rock garden culture during the early 1930s. These containers were usually no larger than 12 in. (30 cm) and created in a similar manner to the English slab gardens. The base was provided by a specially-treated wooden box on which rocks, agglomerates, or tufa were affixed. The space between the rocks was then filled with the plants. This method provided remarkably attractive miniature gardens which could be placed in appropriate locations, even in a window. In 1936, Karl Foerster related in his book *The Rock Garden of the Seven Seasons* approaches to creating miniature rock gardens for window boxes and wooden containers, as well as references to portable miniature gardens in specially-made, durable bowls. Foerster indicated the nearly inexhaustible possibilities for using hardy plants in the garden and in protected areas near the house, be it a balcony or a roof patio. He also remarked how sad it was that there were so few miniature rock gardens and window boxes. Foerster believed that for such locations greater possibilities for using plants existed than anyone had imagined. Only after the war, though, did Foerster's hopes become reality.

But first back again to England. Largely due to the very popularity of container gardening and the use of alpine flowers and other plants, stone troughs and containers became very scarce. There was even a shortage of tufa, which is so useful in rock garden culture. Eventually an artificial tufa was invented. Sphagnum peat, sand, and cement were mixed to make a porous material that had many of the attributes of natural tufa. Of course, construction industry experts scoffed at such a combination, and would not believe that the acidic sphagnum and the alkaline cement would mix without any reaction. However, experience has shown that this is indeed the case. This so-called hypertufa mix was used initially to replace natural tufa. Soon, though, the mixture (with a slight adjustment in the proportion of the ingredients) was also used to mold entire troughs and other containers. Properly finished, such hypertufa troughs can scarcely be distinguished from the real thing. Algae, moss, and lichen soon grow on it, whereas a typical concrete container requires years of outdoor exposure to lose its smooth, unnatural exterior and acquire the patina of age.

At one time, concrete troughs were not considered acceptable for the culture of plants—especially alpine plants. In the interim, we have come to realize that the material the vessel is made from is of secondary importance. Stone or concrete, wood or plastic, makes little difference to the plant and its growth habits.

More recently, the concept of a more mobile garden has contributed greatly to the development of a bit of nature on every patio, terrace, or balcony. Instrumental in this development has been the gradual diminution of garden plots in modern times. At the same time, however, the concept of "garden" has remained alive, only in the form of smaller, portable plantings on patios or even in window boxes. This has permitted different, more creative approaches to gardening than before. As a consequence, many gardeners have found that the pleasure of the overwhelming but short-lived bounty of summer flowers is no longer sufficient. They desire a real piece of nature, a permanent plot they can enjoy all year long, one where they can view the change of seasons, and one that allows them to feel that life is stirring, even in deepest winter.

This approach to natural beauty and a different, more intensive, form of gardening does not mean that such gardeners are willing to give up decoration and color—one only has to consider the rock garden ornamental shrubs, so appropriate for a decorative, perennial display. The beauty of alpine and rock garden plants, considerably more reticent and delicate than larger, showier plants, makes them small jewels.

Let me sketch out the differences, since these also have a bearing on possible approaches: rock garden perennials to a considerable extent really do come from alpine regions. Moreover, they are sufficiently robust to flourish in gardens without undue special effort on the part of the gardener. For these plants, rocks are decorative additions, not essentials of life. They are hardy and durable, bloom readily, and are colorful. Alpine and montane plants in the garden do, how-ever, require human assistance. They have special requirements (for example, proper drainage and protective rocks) without which they succumb. They demand close attention. Each plant is a solo performer. Such plants make chamber music, while the rock garden perennials perform as part of an orchestra. Who could deny that each type has its own special satisfaction?

For the lover of alpine plants, no other form of gardening has a greater attraction than recreating a bit of nature in a window box, a trough or a container and watching the plants develop. There are many creative opportunities around the garden or the home for such endeavors. Let it be said, though, that a great deal of love for the plants is required for the successful care of such miniature gardens. The world of alpine plants opens its doors only to those gardeners who are knowledgeable and willing to adapt. The magical attractions of this inexhaustible treasure-trove of plant varieties can be captured best in such a rock garden or a small container garden.

Thanks to modern methods of cultivation it is considerably easier to tend these lovely treasures of nature than in earlier days. This fact contributes to the trend toward ever-greater utilization of hardy miniature gardens, as an increasing number of plant lovers discover the rich world of alpine plants and the modern means of growing them.

Design Options

General Principles

All alpine miniature gardens have one characteristic in common: the growing medium is quite distinct from the underlying base, no matter how many layers and combinations of soil material the vessel contains. This fact is as obvious in slab or trough structures as it is in miniature rock gardens, rockeries, or similar displays—the growth medium is isolated from the substrate. This isolation results from the coarse gravel used as a drainage layer in the bottom in all miniature gardens. On terraces, patios, and balconies, the use of perlite or absorbent clay serves the same purpose but with lower weight. This separation from the substrate is the first pre-condition for successful cultivation of alpine plants. With such drainage, the desired plants and perennials can be planted in very specific growing media and are thus given virtually ideal conditions for development. Of primary importance here is perfect drainage. Any superfluous moisture must be allowed to drain away, as retained moisture will kill many alpine plants. When one has provided these basic requirements—namely proper and sufficient drainage and a light, airy, and permeable planting medium—alpine plants can grow and flourish in all sorts of vessels and miniature gardens.

For aesthetic reasons one should pay heed (especially with hardy representatives of montane plants) to the harmonic relation between the plant and its container. The fullness of summer flowers fits more appropriately into some unusual vessel than the more restrained and noble reticence mountain plants seem to have. With a little understanding of the mountain plant's nature, it should not be too difficult to achieve a well-balanced whole. Once again, the Far East provides the model for displaying alpines. The imitation and presentation of nature in a small space has made the Chinese and Japanese masters of the style, be it in a small garden setting or container, of the art of the harmonic interaction of vessel and plant; witness the Japanese bonsai treescapes or the Chinese penjing. It is of utmost importance that one combine vessel, plants, and location in a natural manner when designing and installing hardy miniature gardens. If the gardener observes these fundamental aesthetic and material requirements, then the way is open to choose among a nearly inexhaustible number of possibilities and alternatives in garden design, including even the numerous formal design options.

The Classic Form:
The Trough Garden

The classic miniature garden is the trough. Though a small trough may suffice for the year-round display of single alpine plants, a larger one is more appropriate for gardeners desiring to bring a piece of nature to a patio or balcony, especially so for those without an adjoining garden. For proper plant growth neither the size nor the form of the container is important. However, the depth of the vessel does play a role as some species require a fair depth of medium. Shallow depths permit the soil to dry more quickly. But the selection of plants suitable for trough culture is so great that even shallow troughs and sinks with depths of only 4 or 5 in. (10–12 cm) are just as useful as shallow trays. Of course, old, stone livestock watering troughs, such as unusual pig troughs or cattle stone sinks with the ironware still attached, are the most desirable. Occasionally one is able to find a discarded wooden trough. In old smithies, a stone water trough was needed to cool hot forged metal. Such artifacts make superb vessels for an unusual garden design. It does not much matter whether the trough was hewn from limestone or sandstone, although limestone *is* usually a bit more fragile. Nor need the gardener shy away from broken troughs, since the pieces can be reassembled in their final location. Often they do not even need to be cemented, as long as the substrate is solid, as alpine plants enjoy such cracks and nooks—such an ancient container soon presents a realistic and natural appearance. Troughs without any bottom may even be used. One can recover rock window or door frames from many old farmhouses or urban dwellings. Placed upon an appropriate base, they make good trough substitutes. When in the country keep an eye out for suitable troughs, although major finds are becoming rare nowadays.

Other options exist. Troughs and vessels made of concrete are perfectly

Old watering trough, planted with alpines and dwarf conifers.

Even a low stone sink can be used for planting.

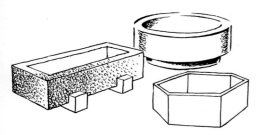

Concrete troughs of different shapes found in commercial garden centers.

A hollowed-out tree trunk is an excellent container for planting.

acceptable, as are those made of other materials. We can today choose from concrete troughs in practically every shape and dimension—square, rectangular, or polygonal. A trough made of washed concrete fits nicely into the patio layout of a modern home. Most manufacturers maintain a wide assortment of troughs made of concrete, sandstone, or limestone. Concrete troughs are just as suitable for the display of alpine plants as old stone watering troughs. In fact, the concrete trough has the advantage of being readily available and of being just the right size.

In modern apartments and houses good architects aim to include provisions for plant placement on balconies and garden terraces. These are suitable for miniature gardens without further modification—so long as no mistakes are made thereafter. All too often the contractor provided only sub-soil for landscaping, as the result of bulldozing the site. Such soil is neither suitable for a garden nor a trough medium. The correction of sub-soil deficiencies can require much effort and cost. Use only materials such as peat, sand, perlite, and the like when installing a permanent planting of hardy varieties of alpine plants.

Clearly, not all troughs are made of stone or concrete—wooden vessels can work as well. A hollowed-out tree trunk, an old wooden spring holding tank, a halved wine or whisky barrel, or even an

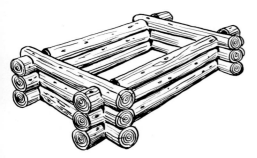

Plant container built out of notched logs.

A trough hewn from a conifer log has special appeal.

old bakery bread mixing trough are all suitable for growing plants. Particularly effective are plant containers built from round logs. In these cases, though, it is important that the wood be treated properly so that it remains durable beyond its natural life-span. Barrels are very durable but require special attention to fit properly into the general garden design and surroundings.

Plant troughs should always be elevated. The container gains visually in appearance and lightness and is closer to the observer's eye. In addition, drainage is improved.

Frame for a Slice of Nature: Slab Gardens

Slab gardens were developed to show more plants on a larger surface than was possible in a trough garden, and the viewer could observe the plantings more comfortably and more clearly. However, it soon became apparent that the flatness of the enlarged planting was visually unappealing, unlike trough gardens. Miniature slab landscapes demanded some sort of topographic design and natural detail. Indeed, it is now apparent that only slab gardens are suitable for designing true alpine miniature gardens, where small verdant valleys are separated by rocky ridges in which an old rootstock is planted to lend character.

A slab garden can be placed just about anywhere—on terraces and patios, in the atrium, in a special site in the garden—and it can be the focal point or provide the background in a stunning garden design. This type of container garden is well-suited to the cultivation of small and rare montane plants, and if the design of the garden is well done, much satisfaction is offered the viewer. In trough gardens a single plant is typically the focus, interacting with rocks, other plants and its surroundings. The slab garden on the other hand is almost always designed as a coherent landscape with dwarf conifers or shrubs providing accents. In such a design alpine plants are fitted in and complete the display. However, the danger of over-designing is always present, and all too often one finds garden gnomes, figurines of cows, deer, other animals, and perhaps a miniature cabin in such a tableau. The more natural and plant-oriented the design, the more successful it will be.

Slab gardens can be created from many materials. While the first slabs were quite simple—legs of cinderblock, the edge made of brick and mortar—the design was soon improved.

Cement trough placed atop U-shaped concrete supports.

Slab garden on a base made of U-shaped
concrete blocks. The edge here is made of
decorative brick.

Slab gardens are also appropriate for
presenting alpine plants in the tiniest of
spaces. Alpine plants enjoy better
growing conditions in slab gardens than
in small troughs. As with troughs, growth
does not depend on the material used in
or the size of the container. The possibilities for natural design are greatly
expanded as slabs are particularly well
suited to forming topographic features
with the soil or building imposing rock
formations. And they possess that feature
absolutely essential to the general well-
being of alpine plants: good drainage and
an airy, permeable plant medium suitable
for various plant species. Continuing care
is also easy since all parts of a slab garden
are readily accessible, and one need
hardly bend over to cultivate them. An
additional advantage is that nearly all
details can be readily seen by the
observer.

Ground-Level Miniature Rockery and Alpine Garden

The common element of these forms of
small gardens is their positioning—
directly on top of the soil surface; however, they must possess an effective gravel
layer for proper drainage. They also share
another trait: these gardens are visually
more appealing if located against a wall
both for support and for outlining the
plantings in a dramatic way. But this
preferred placement does not preclude
the installation of successful free-standing
miniature gardens. Ground-level rockeries differ from other design forms in that
a rockery is a type of garden in which
single rocks or groups of boulders merely
serve a design function and are not in
themselves necessary for the proper
planting of the chosen alpine flora. For
instance, rockery shrubs are not directly
dependent on a rock, as is the case with
alpine plants. For the latter species an
alpine or rock garden is preferable. In
such gardens rock is a requirement for
cultivation of alpine plants in order to
mimic the natural surroundings from
which they came. Excellent drainage, once
again, cannot be stressed enough.

As described in greater detail in the
following chapter, miniature gardens are
usually edged with a low rock or wooden
border. In all other respects they are then
designed and planted like a trough or slab
garden.

There are few other areas of a garden
that can be planted with such great variety
or which draw so much attention as a
miniature alpine or rock garden, especially one designed so that at least part of it
receives some shade. While it is desirable

A rock garden is created from many rocks and alpine plants nestled between the pieces.

for such gardens to be well-illuminated, location in hot, sunny areas is best avoided.

The cultivation of particularly difficult and rare montane plants seems to be most successful in what some call "cliff gardens". Tufa and odd-shaped limestone boulders are generally preferred for the construction of cliff gardens, although irregular rocks composed of sand or limestone may also be utilized. These rock walls, normally supported by a stable wall invisible to the casual viewer appear just like a rock pile in nature. They also provide ideal growing conditions for alpine plants. Gardeners intent on raising rare and tender varieties can cover the plant collection with translucent plastic when special protection becomes necessary. This is not at all difficult and provides the advantages of a miniature conservatory for the moisture-sensitive and thus more demanding plants of the higher elevations. For these a simple cover with good air circulation may be a completely satisfactory—and often even the preferable—solution.

Wall Garden and Raised Bed

Another, very promising possibility for alpine plants is a wall garden, so popular in England—an alternative is the raised bed. Wall gardens are stone structures of some regularity and form. They may reach heights of 1–2 yds. (1–2 m). Their width at the bottom is also nearly 2 yds. (2 m), and the stone walls are angled slightly toward the center of the structure for better support. As a consequence, a small plateau is created at the crown, perhaps a yard wide, which offers minimum possibilities for planting, in addition to all the niches created in the two walls. If at all possible, wall gardens should be oriented along an east-west axis to permit both a sunny and a shaded area. In England they are often located directly in the center of a lawn area and are thus accessible from all directions.

The real secret of a wall garden or a raised bed is excellent drainage, mostly due to the rock and gravel core. There is almost no better or more comfortable place for alpine plants than in a well-

The wall garden is built like a dry-stone wall.

designed wall garden or raised bed. The latter can be made somewhat broader than the wall garden, but should be no higher than 2–2½ ft. (50–80 cm). Raised beds are usually made of evenly-hewn rocks and thus fit well into the general design of a home, or the border of the walkway to the front door or a terrace.

A raised bed is attractive near the house.

Natural: Limestone Blocks

The most natural alpine garden, without a doubt, is created by transplanting hardy alpine plants directly into pockets in rock. Where limestone is common one can find unusual boulders perforated with holes or full of erosion-caused depressions and hollows. This damage to the rock face is caused by weathering: the softer lime has been washed away, leaving the harder, more durable limestone. Rocks of this sort are available in all sizes, and look attractive even without plants in them. Small alpine plants are especially comfortable in the hollows and interstices. The holes and cracks are ideal growing areas for alpine rarities such as Alpine Woodruff, *Acantholimon graminifolium*, or *Lewisia*. When mats and vigorous pillows of plants appear, and when *Sedum* or *Saxifraga* squeeze into the irregularities, the plant lover will always find a satisfying scene.

Fill the indentations and holes of such rocks with a light, porous soil. Directions for transplanting alpines are found elsewhere in this book. A good support for a single limestone rock is a thick stone slab; an old, round millstone or grinding wheel; or perhaps even a thick round from a large log. Two or more pieces can be fitted together easily on an appropriate base in order to create the appearance of a single, larger rock structure. The inevitable spaces between the rocks provide additional planting spaces.

Several limestone boulders make a fine rock garden.

Attractive and Useful Window Boxes, Containers and Pots

Those growers who think the creation of a miniature garden too costly and time-consuming—or those who have little display space beyond a window or a balcony—need not give up any thought of a hardy outdoor garden. Even a window box or a container on a balcony is suitable for such plants. Usually, a 6 ft. (15 cm) wide box is sufficient, although an 8 ft. (20 cm) width is preferable. The material—whether plastic or wood—is of little importance, except that wooden boxes should be treated to improve their durability. Such boxes can be planted with dwarf conifers, between which summer-flowering container plants can be set out in spring, or alpine plants, grown to establish collections of hardy perennials and alpines.

Apart from boxes, smaller vessels, such as pots or other round containers, are also well-suited for miniature gardening. These vessels need only be able to withstand weather and the effects of frost without damage. Such containers can be designed very attractively, for example with a natural dwarf conifer, at whose feet pillows and mats of ground cover can

Even a single limestone boulder looks attractive when inhabited by interesting plants.

Window box planted with perennials.

spread so as to eventually grow over the edge of the container. Such plantings are very attractive and can be placed wherever there is open space, but never indoors as artificial heat and indoor air harms most alpines. Only few can thrive in a container near a window indoors and are best left to the expert grower.

Planters to be used out-of-doors the year round must be made of frost-resistant materials.

Construction of Miniature Gardens

Location and Surroundings

Alpine plants must be sited in keeping with their characteristics. For instance, if shade-loving plants (such as dwarf rhododendron species or alpine violets) are selected, then the trough garden cannot be set out in full sun. By using slab garden methods judiciously one can create areas of light or partial shade in otherwise sunny locations. In most cases, however, troughs and slabs are located in bright, sunny areas and so must be planted with sun-loving plants. Good sites, for both effective garden design and plant performance, are patios, beside evergreen hedges, or in front of walls and fences. A larger collection of troughs can provide a border along a path, especially when the path separates the lawn from flower beds. Placing containers in or at the edge of the lawn area creates the problem of mowing around them. One remedy is to place flagstones or slabs under or around the containers. One can also place the containers along a widened stretch of the path so that they no longer stand on grass. Usually, it is simpler to pave the area than to trim the grass around the container by hand. A layer of gravel or crushed rock may serve the purpose as well. Another practical consideration is the matter of irrigation. It is a good idea to combine the construction of a miniature garden with the installation of a watering system. This will be discussed in greater depth later in this book.

Preparation of Used Vessels

In order to use a beautiful, old, stone trough, drain holes must be chiseled or drilled in the bottom. Chisel drainage holes into the vessel's underside by turning it upside down. A simple cold chisel, preferably a round one, and a small mallet or heavy hammer are the only tools needed. Do not rush the job! Slowly chisel out a good-sized hole in the bottom of the trough. It should take only 20 or 30 minutes even if the bottom appears impregnably thick. The final chip is usually cone-shaped and so creates a concave opening on the inside of the trough. A drain hole must be of sufficient width to prevent it from being clogged with debris, which is why I suggest using a cold chisel rather than a drill. A masonry drill makes a narrow, straight-walled opening, easy to clog and making it necessary to drill several holes. The larger the drain opening, the better the drainage.

A broken or heavily damaged trough can be reassembled directly on site. Such troughs are more easily obtained than whole ones, but little additional effort is required to reassemble the pieces. With a proper base the pieces can be fitted together with little worry that they will fall apart once they are planted. Indeed, the existing cracks provide better drainage. Soon, the cracks and crevices will be home to several plants. *Campanula cochleariifolia* (syn. *C. pusilla*), the Alpine Bellflower, is exceptionally well-suited for this purpose and creeps into crevices with ease. A restored and fully planted trough makes an especially interesting display.

Old stone trough with pouring lip, placed atop flagstones.

Homemade "Old" Troughs

For the real devotee, nothing can compare with an ancient, perhaps well-weathered, stone trough. But where can most gardeners find these today? Fortunately, there is a method by which one can create "old" troughs, and the effect is more than worth effort. The method originally came from England at a time when it was thought that concrete troughs and other such vessels were not suited for proper cultivation of alpine plants. At the height of the passion for old troughs it became clear that the supply was limited. In searching for a usable substitute for tufa, a mixture of peat, sand and cement was developed; eventually, it was found that this mixture could also be used to make troughs. Such homemade containers weather so well outdoors that within months they are virtually indistinguishable from ancient, weather-scarred stone troughs. Moreover, I know of troughs of this type that have withstood all sorts of wind and weather for over 20 years and promise to last even longer, all detractors' comments notwithstanding. After a period of years weather does take its toll; frost damage may cause a piece to split off the exterior of the shell. But this only makes the trough look even more authentic—and in any event, old stone troughs also suffer weather damage. If the ingredients are mixed properly, then weathering will not lead to premature destruction of the trough.

Materials and Dimensions

Material. What eventually looks like real, aged rock is actually a mixture of peat, sand, and cement. The proportions of these materials influence the characteristics of the finished product. If more cement is added to the mix, the trough is more stable but heavier; also, it will look more like limestone. A greater proportion of peat yields a finish similar to sandstone and also makes for a lighter and more porous trough which permits easier passage of air and moisture. But such a mixture is more subject to weathering during the winter, thus reducing the trough's usable life. A mixture of two parts peat, one part gritty sand, and one part cement may be perfect for the creation of imitation tufa, but the results are too porous and weak for a substantial trough.

Tests with different combinations of mixtures indicate that the best proportions for creating durable troughs are achieved with a mixture of 2 parts peat, 3 parts sand, and 2 parts cement. A plant trough created from such a mix and then finished properly gains a weathered "old trough" appearance within days. The results are striking—some troughs replicate the real thing so well that one has to look very closely to tell the difference.

Dimensions. Before constructing a mold in which to cast troughs, one must be certain that the dimensions stand in correct proportions, that is, length, width, and height have to be in an eye-catching relationship and correctly reflect the space into which the trough will be placed. The relationship between width and height deserves particular attention. The length of the trough, on the other hand, may be varied more easily. Following the relationships of the Golden Section will always produce a well-proportioned trough. But good proportions are not everything. It is very important to provide sufficient depth to permit the plants adequate space for root development. The following sizes have proved to be extraordinarily handy and not too heavy to transport easily:

Several troughs placed end to end along the edge of a path make an attractive border.

24 in. long × 14 in. wide × 11 in. high
(60 × 35 × 28 cm)

31 in. long × 16 in. wide × 11 in. high
(80 × 40 × 28 cm)

40 in. long × 18 in. wide × 11–12 in. high
(100 × 45 × 28 cm)

The last is considered the ideal size, and a standard measurement whose length may be increased as desired without any change in height and width. Troughs up to 7 ft. (2 m) long have been produced and are especially eye-catching. However, due to their considerable weight they must be molded in place.

Construction

Forms Made of Wood or Cardboard. Once the dimensions of the trough have been determined, the form can be prepared. Only basic skills are required, and measurements need not be absolutely accurate just as old stone troughs were not precisely cut. In truth, the more closely the form approaches a homemade appearance, the more authentic the trough will look.

Suitable materials for forms are scrap lumber, rafter boards, or cardboard cartons. If using a thin-walled paper box, another entirely acceptable material, and the walls bend outward during the pour, the resulting trough will only gain from these irregularities, looking more authentic by virtue of its imperfections. Wooden boards make dependable material for forms and also have the advantage they can be used again or taken apart for other uses. In time, one can create an entire collection of "old" troughs of varying lengths by simply altering the placement of one of the end boards.

The easiest form to prepare is the cardboard carton. For smaller troughs consider banana boxes, which have the additional benefit of having useful dimensions. But considerably larger boxes should not be ignored. Provide proper support for the exterior walls with, for instance, clumps of peat, a nearby wall, concrete cinderblock, a few wooden boxes, or whatever is appropriate when using cardboard. A few rough spots are part of the allure of such troughs.

The construction of a wooden form is depicted in the following illustrations. The exterior sides are set on a flat surface covered with plastic, as this design does not use a bottom panel. As illustrated, the exterior boards or panels are nailed together to yield the desired finished dimensions. Be sparing with the nails, as you want to take the mold apart with as little effort as possible. By nailing two sets of clamping boards as shown, one for each end of the trough, unnecessary steps in the construction can be avoided.

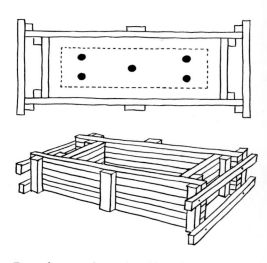

Form for trough, made of boards.

Reinforcement. Once the mold is completed, several other matters must be addressed. In order to strengthen the trough it is necessary to place into what will be the bottom and the sides reinforcing material such as wire, wire mesh or rebars. Scrap metal bars and similar materials can be used if available. Thin metal rods should be bent at right angles to reinforce the corners of the trough. Such reinforcements should be prepared and cut ahead of time, and the more metal used the better. To stabilize the bottom it is best to cut an appropriately-sized piece of wire mesh or chicken wire. One can dispense with such reinforcement in the case of small troughs, but it certainly won't do any harm to the final product if it is used in this case as well.

Drain Holes. Four or five dowels should be cut from an old broom handle or pole and placed vertically in the bottom to provide for drain holes. Since these dowels also provide temporary support for the core form, they must be cut as long as the bottom thickness, usually 3 in. (8 cm) or so. When placed on end in the desired locations for drain holes, the dowels will prevent the core form from sinking to the bottom.

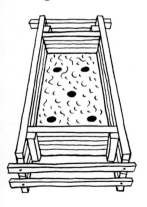

Location of the drain holes in the bottom.

The Interior Core Form. It is best to use a styrofoam block, easily obtainable in larger hardware stores and lumber yards catering to the construction trade. Using a saw—or better still a large ripsaw—cut off a piece that fits the interior dimensions of the trough exactly. These dimensions depend on the desired thickness of the walls. It is always advantageous to ensure that the base and sides of the trough are not overly thin. The base, in particular, should always be thicker than the sides, preferably in a ratio of 8:5. Even with smaller troughs the walls and bottoms should be no less than 2 in. thick (5 cm).

Keep the Separation. To maintain the distance between the wall of the form and the core before and during the molding process, saw spacers in the desired width or thickness of the walls. If planning on using the core form for other troughs of other dimensions, divide the block into two larger and one smaller block. The latter will fit in the middle between the others and can be removed more easily and without damaging the blocks. The dimensions of these several blocks should be calculated and cut to those useful for smaller troughs.

Production and Finishing

Mixing the material. When all required implements and materials have been gathered, the pouring can be started. First, the dry ingredients are mixed. The peat should first be finely-sieved (the more finely-sifted the better). To 2 parts of sifted peat, add 3 parts of coarse sand and 2 parts of cement, and mix thoroughly. The total quantity required obviously depends on the size of the trough. For a planter with the dimensions of 40 × 18 × 14 in. (100 × 45 × 35 cm) and a wall thickness of 3 in. (8 cm) the following quantities are needed:

- 1 construction wheelbarrow (about 20 gallons) of sieved peat (85 l)
- 1½ wheelbarrows of coarse sand, and
- 1 wheelbarrow of cement

This quantity will also suffice for the making of two or three small troughs.

Pigmentation. If a particular color is desired, an appropriate oxide color dye can be added to the dry ingredients and blended in. For each wheelbarrow's worth of mixture, 2–4 oz. (50–100 g) of oxide dye should be added and adjusted to the desired tint. It is easy to vary the color from trough to trough if they are slated to be poured the same day. Although oxide colorants are available in many tints, only red oxide and possibly also brown oxide can be relied upon to provide a natural-appearing color. A trough tinted with red oxide looks like a freshly-hewn sandstone planter. Be aware, though, that such pigmented troughs take longer than untinted troughs to acquire the growth of algae and lichens so sought-after for giving the appearance of an authentic weathered stone trough.

Moistening. With or without colorant, water is added to the dry ingredients and thoroughly mixed. Avoid over-moistening the mixture. A thick, viscous mass is the objective.

Pouring. First the bottom of the form is covered with the mixture and the rein-forcing mesh pressed well into the mass. The dowels prepared for the drain holes are then pushed into the mass as shown in the illustration on page 27. By so doing the trough will have sufficient drainage and

the inner core form will be well supported for the duration of the pour. Once the mixture has reached the top of the dowels, place the core form in the center of the mold on the support dowels. Check the distance of the core form from the sides of the form, and then fill the spaces between. Tamp the mix frequently to avoid air pockets and do not forget to place reinforcement wire mesh or rods into the mixture as it is poured (see illustration below).

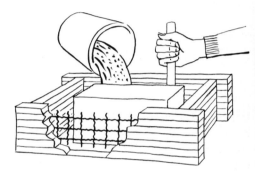

During the pour, tamp the mixture to force out air pockets.

Removing the Forms. The finished trough now has to cure, which requires considerably more time than ordinary concrete. After 48 hours or so carefully remove the exterior form, leaving the core form in place until the exterior finishing is completed. Cardboard molds are usually only useful one time.

Surface Treatment. Now the real work starts: the antiquing of the trough surface to give it a natural and well-used appearance. The material at this stage is still soft and plastic, so the exterior can be easily textured. For this purpose use a medium-hard bristle brush, a flexible spatula and an old, stone cold chisel.

With the spatula smooth the edges of the trough and carefully round off the corners and edges slightly. If a piece should break off here or there in the process, don't fret, for such damage is a definite advantage in creating an old, used appearance. The exterior surfaces are next scored with the spatula in a horizontal direction to remove any trace of the forms. Irregularities may be smoothed out at this time if so desired. In smoothing the grains of sand leave grooves in the exterior, reinforcing the appearance of natural stone. Next use the brush to somewhat smooth the rough features of the trough. At this point the exterior begins to resemble real rock. To perfect the appearance of rock use the flattened end of the cold chisel or the well-worn striking surface of another steel tool to beat the still-soft exterior of the trough, as shown in the following illustration. In so doing, the slight irregularities reminiscent of troughs hewn by stone masons are created. The more indentations, the more authentic the appearance. Now brush all surfaces once again with the bristle brush to round and smooth all edges. The trough exterior should now have a truly weathered appearance. Even veteran trough builders are continually surprised at how authentic and natural such troughs look—just like (or almost like) old stone troughs.

Removal of Core Form and Dowels. The core form which had been providing added stability during the curing and finishing process is removed two or three days after surface treatment, at the earliest. After lifting out the core, remove the dowels from the drain holes but leave the entire trough in place for a week to assure proper curing. In a week or two the trough

can be moved to its final location. Despite careful handling, a few small pieces may break off at the corners. Simply use the brush to round off the corners again—the trough will only gain in appeal. Within weeks of final placement the trough will start to acquire a patina of algae and other primitive plants and so become indistinguishable from an ancient watering trough.

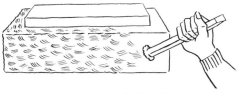

Final finish is done with the chisel.

Elevating the Trough. Always position the trough above ground level using a layer of bricks or cinderblocks to provide a stable base. Whatever is used, the base should elevate the trough 6–10 in. (15–25 cm) and be not quite as wide as the bottom width of the trough. If only two support blocks are used, they should be positioned so as to support the end thirds of the trough. Use a carpenter's level and shims to place in a horizontal position. Make certain that the drain holes are not obstructed by the support material, and reposition the base if they are.

Installation of Drainage Layer

Once the trough is in place, several pottery shards or small stones are placed over the drainage holes to prevent plugging, then the bottom layer of coarse gravel or aggregate, perlite, or similar material is added. The exact material used is not of great importance; just make cer-

29

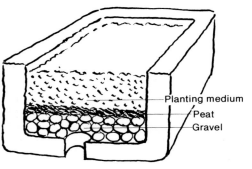

Cut-away view of the trough—planting medium on top, large gravel on the bottom, separated by peat.

tain the material selected is sufficiently coarse to permit thorough, rapid drainage. The depth of this layer depends on the dimensions of the trough; a deeper trough requires more drainage material. A ratio of one-third drainage material and two-thirds soil has proved successful. The soil should be separated from the drainage layer by a 1-in. (2 cm) layer of coarse peat or a sheet of water-permeable landscaping fabric to prevent silting of the drainage layer from above. The drain layer in very tall troughs may reach as high as halfway up the side—for instance in the case of deep balcony or terrace planters. In such situations lightweight plastic containers should be considered in view of the great weight of the trough during transport and the stress imposed on the support structure by such weight.

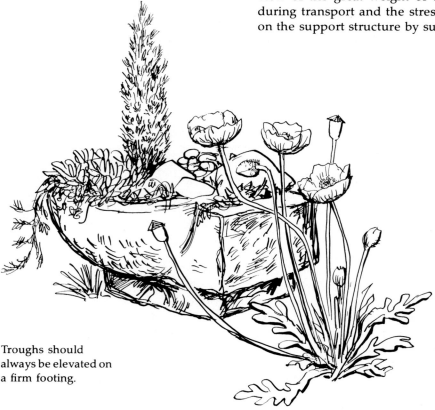

Troughs should always be elevated on a firm footing.

Construction of Slab Gardens

Smaller slab gardens can be constructed out of used splash boards or similar discarded materials. However, they also can be molded to shape from the same mixture of peat, sand and cement used for troughs. In fact, the procedure is nearly the same. I recommend the following dimensions for modest slab gardens: 4 × 2 ft. with a height of 6–7 in. (120 × 60 × 16 cm). It is essential that the floor be at least 3 in. (7–8 cm) thick; the sides may be made a half-inch (1 cm) or so thinner. As with the case of troughs good reinforce-ment with structural metal is called for. The base can be fashioned from U-shaped cement or concrete blocks.

Another approach has proven very rewarding in the construction of larger (and therefore "true") slab gardens—true slab gardens should be large enough that all the options for alpine design remain open. The best size for a slab garden is 6½ × 4 ft. (200 × 125 cm). Commercially pro-duced boards made of fiber glass and mortar are available at construction supply companies and can be used for the bottom upon which I pour 10 in. (25 cm) deep walls.

I recommend the following means of

A smaller slab garden made of exposed aggregate planted in the traditional alpine garden design using limestone rocks.

constructing a slab garden: first a steel frame made of T-bars is required; a sheet-metal or welding shop can fashion one for you (see the sketch below). A frame is made of angle iron in the same dimensions as the bottom panel. This frame is loosely placed on the steel frame and readied for welding. Recheck the layout so that the T-bar frame supports the angle iron frame in the final assembly. Then weld. All steel parts should be primer-coated and later painted with metal paint—green or gray is preferable. For the base use four concrete blocks and level them. Now place the bottom T-bar and angle iron in its final position on the support base. Next, fit the panel forming the base in the frame and drill drain holes with a masonry drill bit—the more holes the better. Now only the construction of the sides remains. Use brick, cinderblock, or clinker cemented together with premix mortar. Lay the masonry to a height of about 10 in. (25 cm) around the perimeter of the bottom panel. After the mortar cures, the slab garden is ready for planting!

Somewhat more costly are walls made of flagstones or concrete panels, neither of which has any particular advantage in this use. However, the steps required to make a slab garden with such walls are somewhat different. While the U-shaped base and the T-bar frame for the bottom is retained, *two* additional frames made of angle iron are required. The open sides of the angle in this case face outward (see sketch below), as these frames support the panels. To do this properly, mounting hooks are installed as shown on the inward-facing side of each panel. The lower frame is then placed on the base, with the hooks over the angle iron. To finish, fit the upper frame over the top hooks.

Frame made of T-bars.

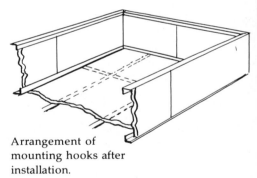

Arrangement of mounting hooks after installation.

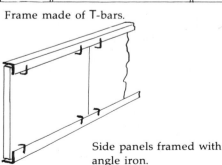

Side panels framed with angle iron.

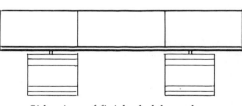

Side view of finished slab garden.

Other materials of course may be used for constructing the sides of this type of container garden and altered at will. However, I caution that good support and stable frame construction be provided, so that the base can take the weight of the garden built upon it. The proper height of the slab garden is predetermined by the cement blocks used. For slab gardens, just as for trough gardens, the motto in placement and location is the same: keep it light.

Once completed and cured, the making of the actual garden can begin. The drain holes drilled in the base panel must be protected from clogging by the placing of clay pot shards and small rocks over them. Next, place a gravel layer about 2–3 in. (5–7 cm) deep over the base, keeping in mind that proper drainage is essential in maintaining a healthy alpine garden, so more rather than less drainage material should be used. In areas where the design calls for elevated spots, additional drainage material is needed as well. This gravel layer is then covered with a 1 in. (2–3 cm) layer of peat or landscaping fabric. On top of that planting medium is spread. The slab garden is now ready for the design elements, rocks or possibly a gnarled rootstock, and then the plants can take their place.

Miniature Rockery and Alpine Garden

The different forms of miniature gardens dealt with in this book are very similar in general construction. All need some sort of border, superb drainage, and if at all possible a wall for support. For the border

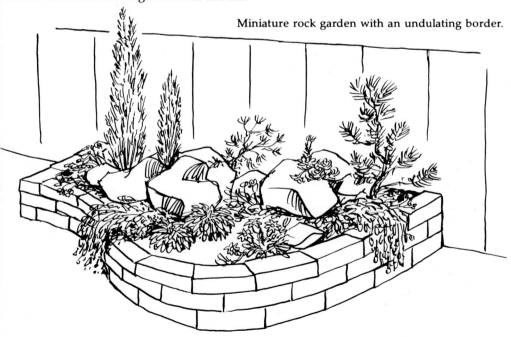

Miniature rock garden with an undulating border.

33

a great number of materials can be used: bricks, clinkers, U-blocks, peeler logs, concrete or cinderblock drain pipes or whatever is deemed attractive. The border should not be too high—8–20 in. (20–50 cm) is sufficient, just about the height of three layers of brick—and it is not even necessary to use mortar for solid construction. These materials are also advantageous because they can be used in a circular or serpentine design, as shown in the illustration below. Rounds or peeler logs, whether installed horizontally or sunk into the ground vertically, must be impregnated with a wood preservative.

Since these gardens are built directly on the ground, close attention to proper drainage must be paid. Commonly gravel is used but may be replaced by other material, such as styrofoam pellets, to lessen total weight in locations where weight is a consideration, such as in roof gardens and on decks. The thickness of the drainage layer is determined by the height of the topsoil above it: the more of one layer, then the more also of the other. In miniature rockeries or alpine gardens the drainage layer should not be any less than 3–4 in. (8–10 cm). In fact, this layer may be spread to nearly the same depth as the border material. The drainage layer is then covered with about 1 in. (2.5 cm) of peat or with landscape fabric, after which the planting medium is placed.

In planning the location of a miniature rock garden or an alpine garden, a dedicated lover of alpine plants will exploit any local conditions that appear promising. First, the right place in the sun must be determined. A rock garden

Boulders give a rock garden its special character.

requires both sunny and shady areas. Secondly, if the rock garden can be placed against a wall—be sure to install a vapor barrier of plastic first—some considerable advantages are gained. For one thing, the width of the garden can be varied as desired. For another, the garden can be constructed to a lower depth. This is desirable for a rock garden that is accessible from all sides, which requires a great depth of material to obtain a sense of elevation. Also, freestanding gardens are more difficult to design than wall-supported rock gardens. Of course one can build up one side of the garden to act as a permanent wall. In this case another side then needs to be built up, with irregular contours to provide contrast; it would therefore be wise to construct a rockery or a raised rock garden from the outset.

A number of large, irregularly-shaped boulders are essential for the construction of a rock garden. Tufa or perforated limestone is ideal. Sandstone or limestone can also be used with good results. Such boulders should be of considerable size—one large rock always looks more attractive than two smaller ones of equal volume. But smaller ones are also needed as the larger look more impressive when seen against smaller rocks. Furthermore, the rocks must be organized in the same direction to give the design a natural appearance.

A rock garden border can be fashioned of brick or evenly-hewn cobbles or rock, 8–20 in. (20–50 cm) high. Alternatively, the border material may be matched to the rocks used in the garden. After the border rocks are placed, the area within the

Several larger rocks look more attractive; the plants soften an otherwise stark design.

border is covered with a layer of gravel or similar material to a depth of 10–12 in. (20–30 cm). A space of 4–8 in. (10–20 cm) is left between the drainage material and the top of the border. This drainage layer may even be increased in the center and toward the support wall, as desired. Once again, the drainage layer is covered with 1 in. (2.5 cm) or so of peat or landscape cloth. Planting medium is then added to a depth of 8–12 in. (20–30 cm). Some of the border boulders may now have to be shifted in order to provide level or slightly sloped planting surfaces for shrubs with shallow root systems. The larger level surfaces should be located near the front of the display, in the lower third, whereas toward the rear and top the planting surfaces will be shallower. Next place the larger garden boulders; a particularly large or striking one might be used to provide a focal point at the rock garden's highest elevation. Be sure to fill all crevices and hollows with topsoil, since these irregularities will become the homes of various alpine plants.

Even if the initial planting does not meet your every expectation, don't fret. Appropriate plants soften the harshest or poorest design, and the entire construction will soon develop a natural appearance. The initial appearance of all the rocks may well be unattractive and cold. But imagine how pleasant the garden will look when carpets of plants have expanded over the rocks and the crevices are filled with wonderful flowers and verdant growth!

A rock garden against a wall or house foundation can easily be covered to provide some protection against the elements. This will expand the choice of suitable plants considerably. Many alpine plants are particularly susceptible to damage from moisture during the winter months when for some of them even excellent drainage is insufficient. By providing a translucent covering, the water supply can be better regulated and a house for the tender plants dispensed with. A temporary, light structure of translucent panels or heavy plastic sheeting is not expensive and can easily be constructed even by amateurs. If the alpine garden is located next to a house foundation wall, the eaves will provide a dry zone. Frequently, a simple construction of plastic sheeting renewed each autumn can help keep winter moisture from affecting sensitive plants. Covered rock gardens should always be covered lightly with snow when frost is expected. Be careful, though, and don't cover the garden with snow to which rock salt has been applied—this is certain death for plants.

Wall Gardens and Raised Beds

Wall gardens and elevated planting beds are ideal for alpine plants. If the wall garden is surrounded by lawn, it is best to provide a pathway of flagstone or cobbles. This path should be designed level with (or better, somewhat lower than) the lawn surface. This permits thorough mowing and edging of the grass. The base of a wall garden should be about 6 ft. (2 m) and the height between 5 and 7 ft. (1.5–2.5 m). An east-west axis is best, since this offers a sunny south wall and a shady north wall.

The first stones should be laid flat, providing the base for the wall. All other courses should be slightly angled toward the center of the structure, much as a retaining wall is built. The structure gains considerable stability by being constructed in this way and, just as important here, moisture retention is enhanced. Rain and irrigation water can enter easily to provide the necessary dampness in the wall interior. Of course, the wall must have good drainage. The entire core should be built as a drainage layer. Together with an appropriate planting medium, the drainage material will guarantee success. Build the drainage layer as the wall is constructed. The space next to the rocks and boulders, as well as the interstices between them, is filled with light, friable plant mediums. This layer extends about a foot (30 cm) inward from the rocks (see illustration). If desired, several particularly striking rocks may be placed on the crown of the wall. Dwarf conifers enliven the level top, to which low-growing ground covers shielding small flower bulbs can be added.

Raised beds are created much like wall gardens. Like the latter, raised beds are ideally located along an east-west axis, but they are considerably lower—usually no higher than 20–30 in. (50–80 cm). However, they may be as wide as desired. Once again, the secret is careful attention to drainage. One-third of the core height should be composed of coarse gravel or small rocks, and drainage is even better if half of the interior is such material. If the bed is very wide, several large boulders may be set on the level top. The length of such a raised bed is determined by the location and the design objectives. By varying the composition of the planting medium along the bed, very different habitats suitable for different plants can be created. For instance, a talus zone for plants thriving on talus cones might be placed next to a zone for hardy orchids.

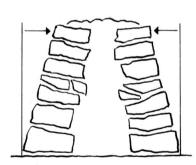

In constructing a wall garden, the sides are angled toward the center.

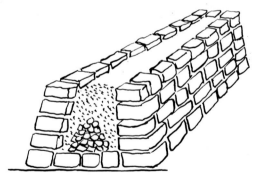

The core of drainage material in the center is particularly important.

Planting and Plant Care

General Conditions of Growth

The alpine plants in our gardens come from all corners of the globe and have very specific demands. Plant lovers well skilled in growing alpines invariably acclimate alpine plants they have collected or purchased before putting them in their permanent locations. As is common knowledge, many alpine plants are protected so one cannot collect them from the wild. The same really should apply to plants not specifically marked for protection. People who persist in collecting usually try to transfer the soil along with the plant thus removing already limited quantities of soil in the erroneous assumption that this will guarantee success at home. In most cases transplanting fails, so that damage to the native habitat is compounded by failure in the garden. More important than native soil to the sustained growth of the plant are the interdependent influences of climate, soil and drainage.

Climate

The macroclimate of a general region and the microclimate in the vicinity of the plant are critical to plant growth. Changes can be made in the microclimate of our garden, but other important climatological factors are beyond our influence.

What *can* be changed, though, is the soil; it must be adapted to prevailing general climatological conditions. This explains why plants transferred directly from their original habitat usually do not do well even when rooted in sufficient soil taken from their native regions.

Soil

Not at all new, but still not adequately acknowledged, is the notion that the physical (structural) characteristics of the soil are of greater importance than its chemical composition in growing alpine plants. Among other things, this means that the division of alpine plants into "alkaline-loving" and "acid-loving" groups is given far too much attention. Long-term observation has shown that only a very few plants are absolutely acid-loving or gravel-friendly. Historically, few of the scientific efforts in the field of alpine flora were grounded in practical procedures; thus in large part the growers were the ones testing and propagating these assertions. These growers argued that plants known to be harmed by alkaline soils could generally adapt to such soils in a garden if the physical characteristics of the soil were right. Nearly all soils contain some traces of limestone. Accordingly, there are very few alpines that are unable to flourish in alkaline soils. Swamp and bog plants may belong to this group.

For most alpine plants, the following guide is sufficient: All plants depend on friable and humus-rich soil. Acidity-alkalinity values are considerably less important. In short, the physical properties of the soil have to be well-balanced; the chemical influences play only a secondary role.

Soil permeability is essential for good growth of alpine plants. In the description of different types of miniature gardens, I drew attention to the importance of proper drainage. But good drainage is not the sole precondition for good growth. The planting medium also has to be appropriate for the task. A mixture for miniature gardens must permit easy percolation of moisture downward to prevent pooling and retention of excess water. Compare this condition to that of a sponge: this water collector soaks up moisture until it is saturated, after which any additional water simply runs out. The soil for alpine plants should be similar. It cannot be too wet, and the excess must have a way to run off quickly.

Drainage

Always keep in mind the natural growing conditions of alpine plants, particularly those from higher elevations. During winter dormancy there is virtually no water available in their habitat, since freezing temperatures have turned all water into ice. It is for this reason that proper drainage during winter is vital. During the summer months, it is easy to maintain a dry garden and avoid adding excess water. It is a different story in winter: away from mountain regions, the weather fluctuates so snow, rain, frost, and thaw alternate in rapid succession.

Garden soil cannot dry properly under such conditions and so remains drenched. Freeze/thaw periods with their change from frozen to moisture-laden soil make it difficult for the more sensitive plants from higher elevations to survive. The cold weather does not bother them since many grow in crevices in the mountains, in nearly vertical rock surfaces where no snow can cling to protect them. Such plants, therefore, also have to survive drastic swings in temperature between day and night. And yet, what a sight when (for example) a rock jasmine is so covered with bloom after all these hardships that not even a sliver of the plant itself is visible below it! Only very few alpine plants die in the garden due to inclement winter weather. The cause of death is usually moisture.

Uniform Soil Mixtures

In the past several decades, 10 or more different mixtures have been recommended for the cultivation of alpine plants in order to meet the needs of particular species. This approach is now outdated. Of course, the experience of those superb raisers of alpine plants are not without value, nor has their advice become useless. But since those days rapid progress in the development of new cultivation methods has been made, nowhere more so than in commercial nurseries. Largely for reasons of efficiency, these methods, including the formulation of soil mixtures, have been simplified. Horticultural research supported these practical applications, especially for commercial gardeners. The use of these modern approaches by amateur gardeners largely depended upon their willingness to learn and transfer them to the raising and care of alpine plants. The experience of commercial nurseries is particularly relevant for "mobile gardens". The use of commercial plant growing media in the tending of containers, pots, and window boxes ensured success. Such media are industrial products with a consistent structural composition and a carefully measured proportion of plant nutrients. These uniform media have so improved modern methods of cultivation in the commercial garden world that nurseries can hardly do without them. These same media represent a significant fraction the media now recommended for alpine plants. If a gardener experiences failure using these simplified—or rather, consistent—soil mixes, the reasons are to be found in the use of traditional cultural methods which worked well in regular soil. When such methods are employed with the new growing media and without any adaptation, failure ensues. Properly used uniform soils demand and also cause changes or adaptations in all cultural methods, including watering and fertilizing. This adaptation requires a certain amount of thought and intuition on the part of the gardener.

Substrates for Alpine Plants

For the purposes of growing and maintaining alpine plants, one type of uniform soil mix has proved particularly satisfactory. It depends upon the use of a lighter type of peat, one that has not decayed to the degree typical of normal dark peat moss. Dark peat moss is not as well suited for container use. Among professionals, plant soils are usually referred to as "substrates". A proper plant substrate should not compact quickly when wetted, since this prevents good aeration and inhibits root growth. This is the reason homemade soil mixes, which often include subsoil or well-rotted compost, so easily compact and inevitably lead to the death of the plants grown in them. Death occurs even when peat or sand are mixed in such soils. Soils of this kind are well suited for annuals, but perennials either rot or are badly stunted in such media. Only by removing and transplanting the plants into new, friable soil, will they survive. Yet relocation is exactly what perennial, hardy alpine plants do *not* need. They require a permanent location and as little disturbance as possible.

Plant substrates based on *Sphagnum* peat moss, on the other hand, decay very slowly. *Sphagnum* is derived from moss found in swamps, and has a very porous structure. This characteristic is very important, since air and water can be stored in these chambers. Moreover, *Sphagnum* can hold considerable air even when saturated with water, allowing good aeration of the root zone and the roots themselves. And, of course, moisture retention is excellent due to the same porosity. Once *Sphagnum* peat has filled with water, the excess is shed, but the pores retain a goodly amount of the moisture. Even when the *Sphagnum* appears to have dried out, it still holds some water. This water storage capability, due to high porosity, is reduced only slowly as the peat ages. That is perhaps also the reason why plant substrates based on *Sphagnum* moss are so well-suited for long-lived, hardy, mountain plants. It is therefore seldom necessary over the years to repot plants growing in such soils in order to renew and replenish the growing medium. But be aware: since *Sphagnum* peat contains few nutrients, all nutrients including trace elements for proper plant growth must be regularly added.

Basic Mix for Alpine Plants

A fully usable plant substrate for alpine plants can be made at home as well as purchased. First, the pH balance of the peat must be raised through the addition of dolomite lime to reach an adequate level of alkalinity. Add about 6½ lbs. (3 kg) of ground limestone to 27 cu. ft. (1 m²) of *Sphagnum*. Be sure to mix the ingredients thoroughly. Wait one full day to allow the limestone to interact with the peat, and then add a complete fertilizer. Generally, 2 lbs. (1 kg) of fertilizer is sufficient for good growth, particularly if the complete fertilizer includes the trace minerals so necessary when using peat-based growing media. Here is a very good basic mix which has especially good structural characteristic for alpine plants:

Basic Mix
30 lbs. (13 kg) of dry, fluffed *Sphagnum* peat
2 lbs. (1 kg) of lime
12 oz. (0.75 kg) of complete fertilizer

Based on long-term field experiments at the Alpen Garden in Pforzheim, West Germany, the following medium is recommended for the majority of alpine flora:

Basic Mix A (Alpine Plants)
10 parts of the above basic mix
1 part builder's sand
2 parts perlite or vermiculite
1 part ground basalt or rock

For container culture, add 1 part perlite to this mixture to help aerate the substrate.

Using Basic Mix A, one should have no difficulty in creating planting areas, even for the more sensitive plants of higher elevations. For this reason, I recommend Basic Mix A to novices. Once the collection has grown, and the gardener becomes more expert, other mixtures (namely B and C—see below) will be required. In the beginning, Basic Mix A is sufficient, particularly since it can be customized to meet the needs of specific plants by the addition of appropriate additives. In some conditions, the simple addition of sand suffices to make the soil more water permeable. For specific plants requiring humus, well rotted compost can be added to the Basic Mix.

The reader is cautioned not to simply ignore the plants after placing them in a proper medium, for soil is only one of the factors in the successful cultivation of alpine plants. A continuing devotion to understanding the environment of these plants is necessary to provide the optimal conditions for good growth.

Basic Mix for Rock Plants

High-alpine rock plants are particularly attractive to the expert alpine gardener. They present a special challenge since these often diminutive cushion plants are difficult to cultivate. Some grow high in the mountains in narrow crevices in the rock or adhering tightly to boulders.

These alpine plants are sensitive to moisture in winter, and they do not care for a saturated soil. In their native habitat the water runs off quickly, and the sun evaporates the remaining moisture. The crevices maintain sufficient moisture to prevent the plant rootlets from getting parched, while the crown is protected from moisture since it is typically found near the rock surface, which is warmed by the sun. Small amounts of humus and eroded rock collect in the rock crevices, providing a substrate for the plants. The smallest particles of this rock are eventually washed down, while the coarser pieces remain on the surface. The bulk of the tender plant roots extend into this finer, friable, yet water-permeable soil, while the crown is surrounded by coarser, lighter, and particularly permeable material. The entire plant squeezes itself into the cracks and crevices of the rock face.

These growth conditions must be imitated in a garden setting. This is where finely ground rock has proven such a useful material. And an understanding of such a habitat makes clear why troughs, rock-strewn slab gardens, rockeries, and alpine gardens are so ideal for these plants: with all their crevices they provide living conditions very nearly identical to those in which these plants have lived and reproduced for eons.

The Basic Mix can be adapted to the special requirements of plants that grow in rock crevices. High-alpine rock plants want a quick-draining and well-aerated topsoil. This soil should warm quickly in spring while permitting rapid drainage of water at lower levels. Consequently, one should add coarse, very porous material to the Basic Mix—perlite is well-suited to the task. Frequently, especially in England, vermiculite is recommended. But because vermiculite is sometimes difficult to obtain, perlite, which is widely available, will provide the same effect. The only drawback to this very airy, water- and air-storing mineral is its white color. Those not particularly bothered by this drawback have an ideal amendment to make the substrate for high mountain plants even airier and more permeable. For the most sensitive plants the Basic Mix is amended with up to 50% perlite. If a gardener finds the white color offensive, fine-mesh pumice will serve as well as perlite.

For plant species whose exclusive habitat is the rock crevice, the following plant substrate has proved effective:

Basic Mix B (Rock Plants)
6 parts of the Basic Mix
2 parts sand
2 parts fine-mesh, crushed pumice
0.5 parts ground rock

In smaller containers, add perlite to increase aeration in the substrate. By adding ground rock, or bentonite, it is possible to raise the pH level considerably from that of the normal Basic Mix of peat and sand which is usually lower in pH. Most alpine plants thrive in soils with a pH of 7 or more, so raising the pH balance without adding lime makes rock a useful amendment.

Ground rock is available in the trade. Milled to almost dustlike consistency it is usually of volcanic origin. For this reason the Basic Mix must be amended by coarser material in order to be usable for rock plants. Coarser grades would be more suitable but are difficult to find, so one must turn to perlite, or pumice which includes both fine and coarse particles.

Some growers have recommended using broken styrofoam but it is not really suitable for alpines. In earlier times, ground furnace slag was used as additive, but it is now hard to find, so perlite and pumice—which are very porous and so trap both water and air to support both a moist yet airy environment in the root zone—are the materials of choice today.

Depending upon the plant species and its natural habitat, the Basic Mix amended with these additives by up to 50% of the total volume has proved quite satisfactory.

Basic Mix for Acid- and Humus-Loving Plants

There are a significant number of alpine plants which have adapted to acid soil conditions. Successful culture with these plants demands the replication of such a growing medium. Such a medium is a mixture of 2 parts *Sphagnum* peat and 1 part dark peat without any limestone. It is designed specifically for the culture of rhododendrons and azaleas. This mix, Basic Mix C, is formulated for plants in thick humus conditions:

Basic Mix C
2 parts *Sphagnum* peat
1 part dark, partially decayed peat
2 lbs. (1 kg) of complete fertilizer per cubic yard/meter of planting mix.

In addition, many alpine plants like an acid humus soil. Such a planting medium can be made by amending Basic Mix C as follows:

Basic Mix D (Acid- and Humus-Loving Plants)
3 parts Basic Mix C
2 parts Basic Mix A

For plants growing exclusively in humus in rock crevices, this Basic Mix D should be altered by substituting Basic Mix B for Basic Mix A.

Basic Mix D can also be varied to accommodate the special needs of particular species. Thus for bog plants increase the proportion of *Sphagnum* peat, and for humus-loving plants add more sand or pumice and ground rock.

Keeping a Supply

It is necessary to proceed with a certain amount of intuitive knowledge about the needs and characteristics of the rarest rock plants, so that the growing medium is suitably amended. The devoted plant lover will keep a supply of the different mixes and additives described not only to use when new plants are acquired but also to add small amounts to a plant clump as the original soil settles. With such simplified basic mixes, the gardener need not keep large quantities of different media for the care of alpine plants as was formerly the case. *Sphagnum* moss, dark decomposed peat, complete fertilizer, builder's sand, and one or two sacks of bentonite suffice to start. Once advanced in this way of gardening, one need add a sack of ground rock, some perlite and some pumice. With these basic materials it is not difficult to satisfy the needs of even the rarest and most difficult species. By adding some mix for acid-loving plants, even bog natives, azaleas, and dwarf species of rhododendron can be planted under optimal conditions at any time.

Planting

General Approach

The basic principles of design, the horticultural guidelines, and their practical implementation are quite similar for planting the various types of miniature gardens. The definition of "miniature garden" used here includes all types of containers down to the smallest bowls. I will therefore first provide general instructions followed by the exceptions unique to the different garden types.

The first principle is: Do not plant during hot weather. If that is impossible, plant in the cooler evening hours and then protect the plants for several days with some conifer branches.

Preparation. Cover the drainage holes of troughs or other vessels, add drainage material, then peat or landscape fabric as recommended in the chapter on garden construction. Also, lay out the other materials in the order they will be needed: the appropriate planting medium, rocks, decorative roots or rootstocks, dwarf trees and shrubs, perennials and necessary tools.

Soil. When placing the planting medium, firmly press each layer down with your

A single rock, offset by an odd-shaped root, and a single dwarf conifer with an upright habit provide focal points in this trough.

fist. This moderate compaction largely eliminates the settling of the plant material. As a consequence, much less backfilling will be needed later. For the same reasons, hill the topsoil about 1 in. (2.5 cm) above the top edge of the container walls.

Rocks. The next step is the placement of the rocks and boulders. In the typical garden they are often no more than decoration linking the usual and trite garden plants in a poor imitation of a mountain tableau; in the case of alpine plants, however, rocks are a necessity as well as the basis of the plants' lives and are included for this very reason. The design will be most convincing if it is generous, reflecting the natural relationship between rock and plant. A striking, larger rock can be made a centerpiece or set off to one side. A smaller but equally interesting rock can provide a visual counterpoint to the overall design—one that may be confirmed by a dwarf conifer. The alpine plants will thrive at the base of the rocks and create a carpet that, in time, will hang over the container edge. Alpine cushion plants repeat the form of the boulders, hug the rock faces and squeeze through the cracks made by leaning several smaller rocks against a boulder. By so doing, the crevices and cracks necessary for the cultivation of true rock plants have been created.

Moisture retention is a further function of the rocks. A film of moisture clings to their surface, which is an important water source for the alpine plants; it is therefore best to set larger boulders at some depth in the topsoil. Smaller rocks—especially those placed on the soil surface—heat quickly in the sun to drive the moisture underneath them. Porous rocks like tufa, able to store both air and moisture for the plant roots, are especially desirable for this purpose. Other types of rocks will, however, do the job fairly well if correctly set in the planting medium.

Plants. Dwarf conifers or other dwarfs have first call. Depending on the type and size of the miniature garden, select one, two, or several trees or shrubs with especially desirable growth habits. Dwarf trees and shrubs provide, as do their full-size cousins in the conventional garden, the structure or skeleton of the design. After placing the dwarf conifers and deciduous trees, set one or two creeping, dwarf shrubs at the edge of the vessel; in time they will extend their branches over the side. The finish—in number and size, well-proportioned relative to the dwarf conifers, trees and shrubs—is provided by the alpine plants.

Buy only plants with well-developed root balls. Such plants are better able to grow without going into transplant shock. In those cases where plants with large root balls must be fitted into a restricted space, compress the balls a bit. Better yet, purchase younger plants. It should be noted that older alpine plants with dense root balls may also prove too robust for the intended crevice site. If so, try to compress the ball with care. If this proves unsuccessful, use the procedures described in "Rockery and Raised Bed".

Wetting. Once the miniature garden is completely planted, water it copiously but with care. *Careful* drenching is very important. The fresh planting medium requires more time to absorb water than does ordinary soil. Take great care to water frequently for several weeks immediately following planting, as freshly transplanted plants cannot absorb a great deal of water at any one time. Therefore, repeated waterings in smaller volumes to moisten the planting medium all the way down to the base is preferable. After several watering cycles, the planting medium will settle somewhat so replenish it with fresh medium.

Crushed Rock and Gravel. After planting, place smaller rocks to check the expansion of rapidly-growing groundcover plants into the space occupied by others. Carpeting plants will not only carpet the container to the edge but also creep into the habitat of smaller, more tender alpine plants, so groundcovers must be contained. By directing their growth in this way, they will be forced to expand over the edge and trail down the side of the container. Separate individual plants in the same way.

Lastly, the entire soil surface is covered with rock chips. Although small pebbles may be used, crushed gravel is better. This gravel mulch performs several functions.

Several interesting dwarf conifers determine the general design of this alpine plant trough.

First, it prevents the light, airy planting medium from washing away when watering or during rain storms. Secondly, it retards evaporation. Lastly, it keeps the soil cool for a longer period. In contrast, in winter a crushed rock cover will warm up more quickly and release this warmth slowly downward. So a gravel mulch does much to create a suitable microclimate.

Trough

Use Basic Mix B for planting of miniature gardens, except when growing dwarf conifers and robust rock garden shrubs exclusively. In this case, use Basic Mix C, lightened and made more permeable with coarse sand. In other planting media, add *Sphagnum* peat to slow the growth of larger plants. In a trough, such unchecked growth is particularly undesirable—the plants must be encouraged to maintain their diminutive characteristics.

An alpine garden must contain a large number of expressive, weathered, and craggy rocks. Perforated limestone boulders are very appropriate, since the holes and hollows assure superb growth niches for rock plants. This environment can be replicated by drilling and planting tufa. In both cases, use Basic Mix B or Basic Mix A.

If the size of the trough permits, the edge should be planned so it is overgrown with dwarf shrubs, such as *Cytisus, Salix reticulata,* or even a creeping juniper, such as *J. horizontalis* 'Glauca'. I have already mentioned how the mat-forming plants and their tendency to expand can be controlled. One must be very careful, especially in smaller troughs, to avoid using rapidly-growing plants since they will quickly disturb the balanced relationship of the landscape scene.

Rather than going on with detailed descriptions of planting possibilities, I urge the reader to study the numerous illustrations for suggestions and guidelines.

(1) Readying materials for the planting of a trough according to the plan at the end of the book. Drainage material and soil have been distributed; now the plants are readied. (2) Placement of rocks followed by the planting of shrubs and then the smaller plants. (3) *Sedum* being slowly and carefully inserted in perforated limestone site. (4) In the rock is *Sedum sempervivoides;* at the edge *Helichrysum milfordiae* (Straw Flower), and next to that is *Erinus alpinus* 'Dr. Hähnle'. (5) All finished: the Moss Pink will grow over the trough's edge. (6) The finished trough from another angle, featuring *Sedum* and *Sempervivum.*

Slab Garden

A slab garden is planted in very much the same way as a stone trough. However, the former provides more possibilities to create an attractive landscape. In order to take advantage of its greater possibilities, the slab garden landscape should be given a strong, alpine appearance. For that, a good number of rocks and boulders are needed. Especially well suited for these scenes are craggy rocks such as perforated limestone and tufa.

While placing the planting mix, work toward the intended topographic form. One approach is to create a large hill over the entire length of the slab which is then completed with a rock feature, or in the case of a larger slab design two or three rock formations, separated from each other by ridges and valleys. When such valleys are covered by carpets of ground cover, the rock formations rise out of them like natural boulders from the surrounding greenery. The planting areas and their character must be considered at the time of rock placement. Depending on the plants to be used in these places, particular planting media will have to be used. At this stage of construction, dwarf trees and shrubs must be planted among the rocks. It is easier to transplant the larger root balls of these plants without a hitch at this

Stone trough with a design using rootstock, rocks, and alpine plants.

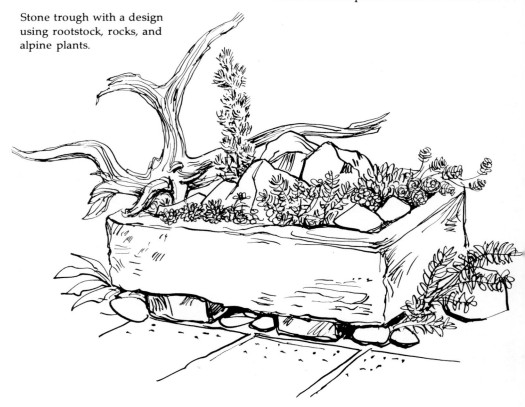

50

stage. It may be necessary to lift one stone or another to make room for these plants. After the trees and shrubs, which give the landscape structure, the smaller perennials should be added.

Orthodox Alpine Garden: The Rock Dominates. A slab garden with a traditional alpine design is a perfect example of how adaptable the style really is. This is particularly true if one has for comparison two slab gardens in close proximity, both in the alpine style, out of one of the traditional kind and the other in the alternative design.

A main boulder dominates the orthodox, alpine slab garden; the plant material is subordinated to it. When rock plays such an important role, designs must appear as natural as possible. This aim is easily fulfilled by using perforated limestone, since this material has almost unlimited possibilities for harboring the most varied array of alpine plants. This opportunity is maximized when the slab garden design is oriented in an east-west direction over the entire length of the slab. Sunny locations then alternate with shaded. Warm, dry areas are found close to cooler places which tend to remain moist when located at the foot of an imposing boulder. The south-facing side can be built up a bit higher by laying several rocks on top of each other. The

A single rock and two columns of dwarf juniper dominate this trough garden.

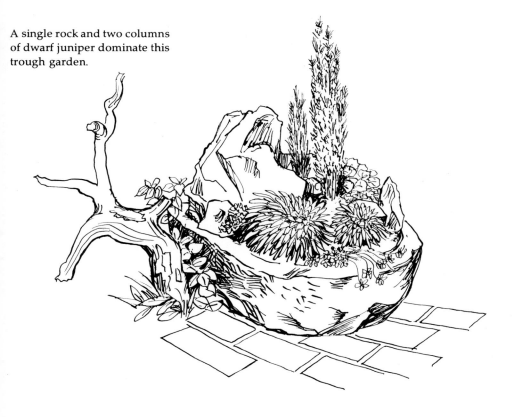

north side, on the other hand, should slope downward. Larger, flatter areas are best created at the foot of the main rock or between several particularly interesting looking rocks. Green mats of low-growing plants can be woven in such areas which also tie the rocks together and give an alpine rock formation a more impressive appearance. Alpine *Minuartia laricifolia*, diminutive *Armeria juniperifolia*, or—in lightly shaded areas—*Saxifraga* varieties are examples of plants useful for such mats.

On a larger slab, the most varied alpine plants can be accommodated if the sites are filled with appropriate planting mix during the rock-work stage. On a base made of Basic Mix A, toward the structure's apex top off with Basic Mix B, especially between the rocks and on the south-facing side. Then a part of the north slope can be filled with a mix rich in humus, the perfect substrate for azaleas, primroses, *Ramonda*, *Haberlea*, Alpine Cyclamen, and fall gentians.

Prepare this humus-rich planting medium using either a mixture of 1–2 parts Basic Mix C and 1 part Basic Mix B, or 2 parts Basic Mix C and 1 part Basic Mix A with an addition of sharp sand. Depending on the plant species, alternative mixture ratios can be created by adding more Basic Mix C or regular peat moss.

In designing a traditional alpine slab garden, one should be guided by the principle of using only dwarf varieties of trees and shrubs, so that the risk of having to remove outsized plants in later years— when they have grown to the detriment of other plants in the collection—never arises. (See discussion of keeping plants, particularly trees, in bounds in a later section, "Training Woody Plants".)

The further introduction of perennials is best started at the edge of the slab garden, proceeding toward the flat surfaces at the foot of the rock formations. Dependable but not vigorous-growing species can weave their mats at the edge. For example, *Phlox douglasii* or *P. diffusa*

(7) This trough made of sandstone and located near the edge of a lawn works well with the flagstone path and at the same time gives an orderly garden design. (8) A fine slab garden. Its secret: the well-balanced relationships among plants, rocks, and wood (here in the form of an old tree trunk). In the background is a Mugo Pine with its verdant growth and gnarly roots. Between rocks, roots, and small clumps of other plants, *Saxifraga longifolia* and hardy Alpine Cyclamen, *Cyclamen purpurascens*, are featured.

are not nearly as invasive as *P. subulata*. In the same space in larger slab gardens, *Aubrieta*, *Saponaria*, and (of course) *Minuartia*, *Lotus corniculatus*, *Dianthus*, or similar plants that tend to trail over a ledge are appropriate. Growth toward the center of the container must be checked by the placing of rock barriers.

Once this initial structure is established, special plants can be added between the rock formations. How beautifully *Aethionema* squeezes into sunny crevices, and how comfortable is the moisture-sensitive American *Lewisia* in a perforated rock, not to mention the *Saxifraga* and Kabschia species. All thrive in alpine slab gardens with high shade and tight rock structures.

For moisture-sensitive species, create a miniature scree slope in an appropriate location. At the bottom of a slight slope, mix the planting medium with some coarse pebbles or pumice. Toward the top, increase the component of rock materials to make the substrate even coarser. When completed, the surface of the planned scree bed will be almost entirely rock and pebbles. Such a site is ideal for *Lewisia*, Alpine Poppy, and a great variety of moraine and scree plants. The sheer

Alpine slab garden with a well-balanced relationship of rocks and plants.

54

number of possibilities to create vastly different growing conditions in a small space is an especially fascinating element of using slab gardens.

Most likely, a gardener will not be able to populate an entire large slab garden at one time. Too much room is left to be planted, and perhaps not all the plants needed are ready for the move. Just make sure to leave space for these.

Alternate Alpine Style: The Plants Dominate. Now to the second approach to alpine landscape design. Here, the rock loses its eminent position and yields to the plants. This approach facilitates fine slab garden design when only a few rocks are available or used. The basis for such a landscape is an admixture of top planting media so some undulations of the surface, hillocks, and valleys, are filled with the planting media corresponding to requirements of the plants used. Miniature conifers now take center stage, backed by several particularly interesting rocks. These two elements together set the tone

A massive rock formation is complemented by a slim, vertical dwarf conifer.

for the design. An unusual tree root accentuates it. The rocks placed singly provide visual support for the plants and tie plant groups together. For this reason, great care must be taken in selecting the dominant plants, particularly dwarf conifers; the species/cultivar chosen is less important here than the features of growth. Nor should the trees be too diminutive. If several different conifers are used, one can emphasize the intriguing contrast between low-growing and upright forms: for example, use a slow-growing type of *Pinus cembra* and a variety of dwarf pine, such as *P. pumila* 'Glauca'. The trees are generally situated on top of, or just below, a hillock, to provide a background. A few, medium-sized rocks emphasize the tree-planted hills. An unusual root, placed under or next to the dwarf pine, may give the appearance of having been the origin of the conifer.

Again creeping, vigorous, carpet-forming plants are well suited for the edge to this type of slab garden. A blue, creeping juniper, *J. horizontalis* 'Glauca', is quite appropriate for this purpose as is Creeping Willow, *Salix × simulatrix*, or a miniature broom such as *Cytisus decumbens*. Several dwarf cushion species provide peaceful green areas in the valleys; during their blooming period, the carpet erupts in colors—*Silene acaulis* 'Floribunda', for instance, is tightly packed with red blossoms.

Different plant groups can be set off by several rocks, and in this way garner additional planting sites suitable for a single plant. True Edelweiss belongs here, as does *Townsendia*, an alpine aster of the Rocky Mountains, or perhaps other single alpine plants. The selection is so great that it is usually difficult to curb a desire to use them all. When planting such slab gardens in which the plants take the main role, it is important to select carefully to provide the contemplative, quiet effect desired. Single plants are displayed better on level surfaces. Several especially interesting plants may be featured or scattered between the plant groupings.

After watering, top dress the soil if necessary and then cover entire surface with a light layer of crushed rock, no larger than pea-gravel size.

Small Slab Gardens. Smaller slab gardens, perhaps with dimensions of 4 × 2 ft. (1.2 m × 0.6 m) are usually designed with level surfaces. Even with a depth of only 5 or 6 in. (12–14 cm), it is possible to create an attractively-styled garden. This is best done by following the design precepts governing bonsai or penjing displays. Using planting medium Basic Mix A, an entire group of similarly sized dwarf conifers can be planted, perhaps a group of three dwarf junipers like *J. communis* 'Compressa', grouped around several rocks. As an attractive counterpoint, use a dwarf elm, *Ulmus elegantissima* 'Jaqueline Hillier'. Between them, an alpine groundcover creates a thick mat, interrupted only by a few smaller rocks.

These are only suggestions for design possibilities—there are no limits on individual creativity in the designing of such miniature landscapes.

Miniature Rock Garden, Alpine Garden, or Rockery

Miniature Rock Gardens for the Novice. Many enthusiastic alpine gardeners got their start with a miniature rock garden. This approach is especially recommended for the novice because it offers larger surfaces for growing less tender, but just as attractive, alpine plants. Yet the more sensitive plants will do just fine in these gardens as well. Their construction requires fewer rocks yet places no limits on the imagination and design objectives of the gardener. The topography of the garden is created using Basic Mix A replete with hills, gentle slopes, and valleys. A gentle, flowing design is particularly advantageous in such a garden and looks particularly compelling after planting.

The choice of well-suited woody plants and alpines is very wide, so one can be extremely selective here. Not all the dwarf conifers incorporated need be low-growing and bushy. A special accent may

(**9**) A showcase for jewels: perforated limestone on a base made of a stone window frame. Both are tied together visually by *Saxifraga cotyledon*. (**10**) This broken window frame was put back together on-site. (**11**) Effective on light-colored rock: dark and reddish *Sempervivum* (here 'Rubin'). (**12**) Planted feeding trough. The light tint of the selenite provides a superb contrast to the dark sandstone of the trough and the greenery. (**13**) A conifer, several *Sempervivum*, rocks—often that is all that is needed. (**14**) Slab garden, partial view: depicting the elements of the construction and the timeless design.

be provided by a vertical, columnar plant. Avoid species that grow too quickly—on the other hand, do not use those that are simply too small. Strive for a well-balanced appearance.

Dwarf woody plants should be located on a hill, if possible, in order to give the visual impression of elevation. At these heights, where special rock plants may be grouped, the rockwork should appear massive, or one may replace several grouped rocks with a single, large and well-weathered boulder. If several smaller rocks are added to the formation, the crevices and cracks can be used for growing the more demanding alpine plants. At the base of the rocks, several creeping plants of a single variety may spread—use at least 5–7 plants, even more if space permits. These grouped plantings will serve as a quiet, expansive surface, supporting the sense of the elevation. Other groups of small rocks tie together other groups of plant species, or prevent unwanted intrusions.

In miniature rock gardens, the image should be one of calm with several plants providing interesting accents, so the plant lover will be able to provide a home for all his plant treasures. Be sure to provide a top-dressing of small, crushed rock after watering the garden down.

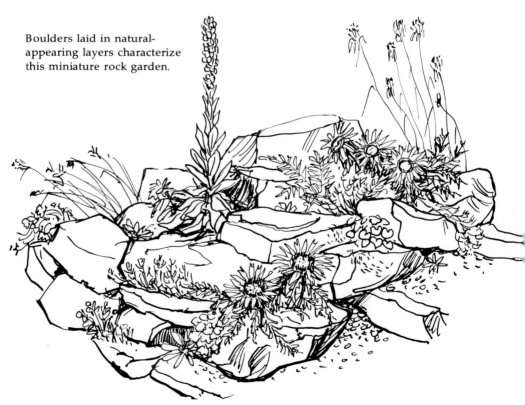

Boulders laid in natural-appearing layers characterize this miniature rock garden.

Miniature Alpine Gardens for the Advanced Grower. The rock garden or the miniature alpine garden is the ideal site for the knowledgeable gardener to grow special plant treasures. By implementing a well-thought-out design, virtually any possibilities can be realized, including those most appropriate for high-elevation plant species.

First, spread a layer of Basic Mix A over the drainage. In the succeeding step, parts of the garden should be covered with planting medium Basic Mix B, principally in sunny spots. In the shaded areas, use Basic Mix C to provide for wetland and acid- and humus-loving plants. For Alpine Primrose, Alpine Cyclamen, or the fall-flowering gentian varieties, add more sand to the planting medium. Most of the high-alpine rock plants are especially comfortable between the sun-splashed rock crevices in Basic Mix B. The Basic Mix A can be moderately varied in the main areas, depending on the special soil needs of the plants used; add sand, peat, perlite, or pumice to the mixture. If all four basic mixes are used for the construction of a miniature alpine garden, and it contains well-lit as well as shaded plant sites, the gardener should encounter no problems in caring for virtually any alpine plant. Lastly, top-dress with crushed rock or furnace slag.

A well-balanced plant selection gives the right look to a rock garden.

Rockery and Raised Bed

When planting the cracks in rockeries and raised beds, one occasionally faces the problem noted earlier, that the root clump of an alpine plant does not fit into the intended site. If gentle compressing of the root ball does not work, shake off or wash away excess soil. Then quickly, before the roots can dry but with great care so as not to damage the roots, settle the plant into its narrow crevice. The plants so set will rapidly recover and grow on in the planting media recommended earlier with little difficulty, and will develop quickly and well. On other occasions, remove some of the planting medium from the crevice and then guide the roots very carefully, with the assistance of a thin wooden stick, down into the crevice—the deeper the better—and then compress the soil around the plant. It is essential to check that the roots are anchored deeply in the crevice, so that the plant is held fast. If not firmly held, the plant will dry out, or rain will flush it out of its site.

Use Basic Mix A, as well as Basic Mix B, in the wall garden. Ideally, Basic Mix A is placed in the lower portion and Basic Mix B in the upper third. By following this plan, the gardener has maximal latitude in his selection of plants. The crown of the wall can then be planted with evergreen, dwarf conifers, preferably creeping types that spread well. Plants with sizable root-balls will also find a good home. It is also possible in the upper portion to lift some rocks, plant larger plants, and then fit the rocks back into place.

In the raised bed, perhaps half of the volume consists of drainage material. Generally, Basic Mix A suffices, but the planting medium can be adjusted in places by adding Basic Mix B, depending on the requirements of the species to be planted. The crevices are planted much as described for wall gardens. The crown of the bed can be reserved for a selection of larger, interesting dwarf conifers.

Dwarf conifers with columnar growth are quite effective in a raised bed, and several plants of dwarf juniper, *Juniperus communis* 'Compressa', or dwarf White Spruce, *Picea glauca* 'Laurin', should be considered. Very impressive groupings can be created with these as well as with various dwarf daphne varieties, *Daphne cneorum, D. sericea*, dwarf willows, dwarf trees and shrubs, and others. In areas protected from bright sun, a selection of dwarf yews, such as *Taxus baccata* 'Fastigiata' (English Yew) or *T. cuspidata* 'Nana', with its slow, irregular habit, are particularly effective.

Limestone Blocks

Limestone is well suited for growing rock plants because of the many holes characteristic of this rock. The holes—which often invade the entire rock, are filled with plant Basic Mix A or B, but do not compact the soil. It may be necessary to occasionally enlarge some of the holes—easily accomplished with a chisel or drill. When an enlarged hole is planted, the soil and the plant will hide any trace of this "unnatural" effort. Enlargements are usually also necessary when holes or other indentations are to be connected with other spaces in order to ensure proper drainage. Care must be taken that alpine cushion plants are nestled entirely within these holes and none of their roots extend into the air at any point. Several rosette-forming *Saxifraga* species, but especially the various *Sempervivum* species and varieties, are also well suited for shallow cavities and indentations and do not require connection with holes in the interior of the rock.

Those gardeners interested in planting such a rock in a more striking way might wish to use conifer or deciduous dwarf tree seedlings and cultivating them in the bonsai style. An appropriately enlarged hole is partially filled with Basic Mix A, after which the root ball of the dwarf seedling is anchored in the cavity. Add more soil and dampen it well. If the rock has several holes on the same surface, the soil on the root ball may be carefully washed away, the several larger roots divided and then planted in each of the holes. Care must be taken to avoid damaging the roots. Anchor the roots very well in the holes, so that the entire plant has good support—the Japanese frequently use a piece of wire to tie the rock and bonsai tree firmly together until the tree has adapted to its new surroundings. Whether dwarf pine or dwarf juniper, the way in which the plant clings to the rock, its roots like claws, makes the plant one with the stone.

Watering such a rock planting is always very important, but particularly so until the plants have really taken hold and are growing well. They should never be allowed to dry out but should, on the other hand, never be flooded or the rock and planting medium saturated. A single rock so planted should be placed in a location with bright, indirect light in order to ensure proper adaptation, after which it can be brought out into full sun. The effort involved in cultivating dwarf trees in a rock finds reward in the interesting highlight or focal point it provides in an alpine miniature garden.

Plant Care

Watering

The care of alpine miniature gardens is really relatively routine, essentially limited to watering. When watering a freshly-planted collection, some care is required until the new roots have developed. Once the plants have acclimated, and are firmly anchored, the workload is reduced considerably. Most alpines are considerably more robust than is generally believed and have adapted to survive extreme weather conditions, as long as they are not subjected to drought. The thick walls of stone troughs and the numerous rocks in miniature gardens provide a substantial buffer against drought, but they cannot compensate for outright neglect. The smaller the area or vessel, though, the more frequently watering is required. Window boxes, planters, and pots require somewhat more attention under these circumstances. The reader should be cautioned that many more alpine plants in cultivation die from over-watering than from drought. These plants are always grateful for a frequent light spraying in late afternoon or evening, particularly so in summer and at lower elevations. This misting reproduces an important climatic factor in their native habitat—provision of moisture without wetting the ground. Obviously, this moisture comes in the form of the heavy dews that develop in the mountains as a result of the considerable temperature differences between day and night. It also occurs as fog resulting from the occurance of heavy downpours followed by sunshine. Thanks to these phenomena, and a water-permeable soil, the plant gains a proper measure of moisture from the air as well as the soil.

Whether using a nozzle on a garden hose or sprinklers connected to an underground water supply system, make sure that the nozzle can be adjusted to yield only mist. There are many excellent nozzles on the market which will supply water from a fine mist to a gentle stream of water. With such a nozzle in the former setting, the plants are watered without soaking the ground. But now and then the garden must be watered deeply, particularly in the warm summer months. From late autumn onward, mountain plants should be kept much drier (see also the section on wintering over).

Pruning and Tending

Further care of alpine miniature gardens is limited to the removal of dead leaves, the pruning away of dead plant material, and the occasional light pruning to shape a plant. Transplanting in the miniature garden should be avoided, since most alpines are comfortable only when they can remain in one place. Carefully transplant only those plants that clearly are not growing well. Some mountain species have a short life span even in nature and so must be replaced at regular intervals. For this reason it is not appropriate to cut off all spent blooms at all times. Apart from the fact that the seed cones and pods of many alpine plants are decorative themselves, the seeds are also useful to start replacement plants. Seeds of rare varieties are usually difficult to obtain and thus are a sought-after commodity among hobbyists who will gladly trade or pay for such seed. Furthermore, many of the alpine plant societies have regular seed exchanges and welcome the receipt of the seed of all manner of alpine plants for their exchanges (see Appendix). Even when the seeds are not harvested, it is a good idea to let a few fall around the parent plant. They may develop into new plants, which then can be transplanted elsewhere.

Alpine plants only need to be fertilized when first being planted. As long as one has used one of the recommended planting media discussed earlier, the plants have sufficient nutrients for at least the first growing season. Alpine plants are very undemanding in this respect. They are not meant to grow lushly; instead, they should maintain the typical tight, restrained habit of rock plants. Accordingly, it is advantageous to keep them a bit lean so as to prevent damage from winter weather. (But see "Window Boxes and Pots" below.) If the media is based on peat, alpine plants benefit from a follow-up fertilization using a soluble complete fertilizer in liquid form. Liquid fertilizer is recommended both because the nutrients are evenly distributed in the solution and because the fertilizer can be targeted to individual plants: dwarf conifers and dwarf flowering shrubs can be watered more deeply, while more sensitive alpine plants can be excluded. Dwarf shrubs in troughs and planters are grateful for such liquid fertilizer after the second or third year in place. The liquid fertilizer should be used only at partial strength—one-half or less the dilution suggested on the label.

The general rule in fertilizing alpine plants is that nitrogen fertilizer cannot be used alone. Fertilizers with proportions of phosphorus and potash are recommended. Thus, lush growth will not be encouraged to the detriment of other plant requirements. Instead, the development of flowers and the hardiness of the plant will be encouraged. Liquid fertilizers with a 5:15:15 ratio are recommended. To repeat: It is more advantageous for plant growth to fertilize more frequently with a weaker mixture than recommended on the package. Do not fertilize later than mid- to late June so that the plants can harden and growth can mature to avoid damage from frosts the following winter. Special fertilizers for alpine plants based on bonemeal mixtures have proven their worth. Late in autumn or in early spring, spread this fertilizer in small quantities among the plants and top-dress with the appropriate basic planting medium. Organic fertilizers are gentle, but their effect is only very gradual. As an alternative, if Basic Mix A or B is added every autumn or spring, any further fertilization during the rest of the year may be dispensed with.

Pests

Generally, few pests attack alpine plants. Mice can be very bothersome: they like to take up residence under snow and pine boughs and then often chew into larger tufts or tunnel underneath them. Combat them with mousetraps or poison-laced grain. Make certain if using poison to place it in the tunnels or cover with a flat rock; then birds and other creatures will not be tempted to pick up the bait.

Keep an eye out for slugs, since even the small species can chew up entire plants overnight. *Campanula* and hardy orchids, as well as all plants with fleshy leaves are their preferred meal. Prevent such onslaughts with slug bait. Most plants survive slug damage and re-grow even when all the above-ground parts have been eaten, but when one is looking forward to a flower's opening, it is especially irritating to see only the naked stem the next morning. Grubs and caterpillars can also do some damage to alpines. Generally they chew off the roots right at the crown so before you know it, a rosette is left sitting on top of the soil, its taproot missing. Grubs can be kept in check with pesticides applied to, or powders mixed into, the soil. Nurseries can advise which of the many brands available is best suited to a particular situation.

Aphids are not normally serious pests in alpine gardens. However, should they multiply quickly on certain plants, there are many means to control them, including that old reliable treatment— soap suds.

Over Wintering

In the autumn, check all plants and trim away all soft and rotting shoots. Plants from which the planting medium is washing away should get a top-dressing of light, sandy topsoil. Dwarf woody plants, particularly evergreen conifers, should be watered well one last time. Alpine plants like to be kept on the dry side during the winter season, but water carefully once in a while even during winter to prevent the soil from drying out completely—but only when frost is not in the offing. Protect south-facing plants from harsh frost and bright winter sun by covering them with conifer boughs, but remove the boughs in spring without delay.

Training Woody Plants

Trunk and branches are the scaffolding of the plant; they determine the dimensions and provide the plant's proportions. Their impact is nowhere more profound than in miniature gardens, where disproportionate dimensions disturb the harmony of the garden and, if left unchecked, may destroy the appearance of the plant. This problem is most likely to occur in rockeries, slab gardens, alpine rock gardens, or elevated gardens. If great care has not been taken to obtain only slow-growing shrubs with clearly dwarf habits, adjustments must be made. In these forms of miniature gardens—in contrast to trough gardens or planters—there is sufficient rooting area and nutrients to allow improperly selected plants to easily grow beyond intended bounds. They are then difficult to keep in check and, in time, if no remedial action is taken, the only option is to remove them, which is usually difficult without also damaging neighboring plants considerably.

A very practical option in keeping conifers short and stout is the nipping of soft spring shoots. This must be done while the shoots are still soft; in no case should they be removed when they have begun to mature. Do not remove the entire shoot appearing in the spring, but leave ½–1 in. (1–2 cm) on the plant. After the damage has scabbed over, the plant will develop at the tip of the cut or break a new bud, which will mature the following year. This procedure must be repeated each year. All pine species—even in the garden—can be dealt with in this manner to develop plants with a low, compact habit. The same method can also be used with firs, spruce, and other needle-bearing woody plants.

The knowledgeable alpine plant gardener will select natural dwarf varieties, that is, plants not needing tending to maintain their diminutive habit for use in troughs and other containers. But plants that are *not* truly dwarf forms in regular gardens can also be used in troughs, etc.,

(15) A non-traditional alpine garden: *Festuca scoparia, Hebe armstrongii, Thuja occidentalis* 'Filiformis'. (16) Garden design element: feeding trough on the lawn next to Oriental Fir, *Picea orientalis* 'Aureo-Spica'. (17) Perforated limestone used with taste and imagination. (18) Japanese Larch, *Larix kaempferi*, in the bonsai style planted in a trough. (19) Small slab garden made of Hypertufa and freshly planted. (20) Dwarves in a trough: an almost 20-year-old *Picea glauca* 'Laurin' next to *P. glauca* 'Echiniformis' and *Pinus cembra* 'Nana'.

16

18

20

65

for in planters offering only a shallow root zone and consequently a more modest provision of nutrients, such plants develop much more slowly. In several years they may reach one-third of their normal size. Prune such plants occasionally to help shape natural growth.

Bonsai-style Dwarf. The effort to influence the growth pattern of a plant is most deliberately realized in the Chinese art of penjing and Japanese bonsai. This really *is* an art whose practice requires considerable knowledge and patience. Despite that, many of its methods—periodic and goal-oriented supply of planting medium and nutrients, pruning of roots and growing tips, the bending and forming of branches with wire and other means for training—are directly transferable to other and more conventional forms of gardening. Anyone interested can develop miniature trees in bonsai fashion in troughs, pots, planters, or window boxes. Nature pursues a simpler and more direct method which can be readily observed any place in the wild, but particularly in alpine settings.

Natural Method. Constrained by shallow, nutrient-poor soils and harsh weather conditions, many alpine conifers that would normally grow into large trees in more placid valleys or plains are stunted in mountain regions. The bare, rocky

A natural appearing design provides a special note to the alpine trough garden.

ground provides little nourishment— only enough to allow them to remain alive. Wind and weather, storm, ice, and snow further abuse these poorly nourished plants in high elevations. Half-starved, bent and broken by snow and wind, and also vandalized by alpine wildlife, the plants tend to remain low, diminutive and gnarled. Despite these adversities, a few particularly tough conifers prevail. Their dwarfed, wildly irregular, often crippled forms remain symbols of adaptation and of the will to live in the eternal struggle against extreme environmental conditions.

Such shaped forms are good models for striking landscape designs. The frame is provided by a small trough or solid planter. Basic Mix A is an appropriate planting medium. It is important that the planting medium has peat as the primary ingredient, for such a medium need not be replaced for years. Again provide proper drainage, and plant a slow-growing shrub or tree—for example, a dwarf conifer. The medium should never be permitted to dry out, a general rule applicable to any planting in shallow vessels or very small troughs. Sufficient moisture is more important than fertilizer. The latter need be applied only after two or three years; the plant will tell when it is time to fertilize. After the roots are clearly established, the gardener can embark on shaping the tree to resemble the tortured but gallant plants of the alpine regions.

With rocks, dwarf conifers, and alpine plants even a windowbox can be designed in the alpine style.

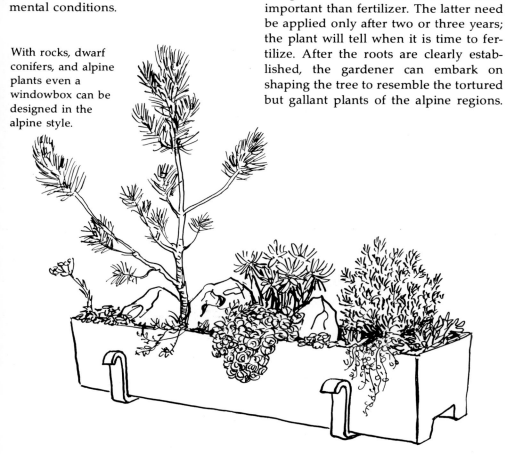

Unlike penjing or bonsai practice, creating such a tree is largely done by pruning with conventional garden pruning shears. Early on, the regular pruning of the small tree is begun. First, remove most of the vertical branches to keep the plant's growth irregular and stunted. Look for branches developing horizontally and encourage such growth. The major pruning is done annually in early spring, just before the buds begin to open. But do not hesitate to prune whenever a branch or sprout seems out of place, regardless of season.

Window Boxes and Pots

Alpine miniature gardens in containers require somewhat more care than the "large" miniature gardens with which they share the details of construction and planting—but the care is essentially the same. I shall cover these differences briefly here.

Of course, good drainage is as absolute a requirement in small containers as in large. It is best to first enlarge the drain holes and then spread a 1–2 in. (3–5 cm) layer of drainage material, preferably perlite or styrofoam pellets, since these materials do not greatly increase the weight of the boxes, pots, or planters. Pea gravel can be used for the same purpose. Just make certain the material is not too fine. Place Basic Mix A on top of the drainage layer. The design typically starts with one or two dwarf conifers, and then proceeds to cushion-forming plants, which are interspersed between them. Two or three especially attractive rocks may improve the general impression if the situation allows their weight.

Plants in such small containers require careful attention to watering, because water evaporates from boxes, planters, and pots more quickly than from troughs or slab gardens. If the containers are located in open sun, even more water is

(21) Clay planter with hardy plants clearly dominating in a picturesque stand of Blue Juniper, *Juniperus squamata* 'Blue Star'. At its base is a special attraction, the gorgeous rosette of *Sempervivum* 'Commander Hay'. At the edge is Moss Campion, *Silene acaulis* 'Floribunda', Rock Sunrose, *Helianthemum scardicum*, and *Minuartia graminifolia*. The planter is brought closer to the eye by its placement on a tree stump. (22) Rock garden made of perforated limestone created at the edge of a lawn with an effective backdrop.

required. Planters filled with alpine plants can tolerate a bit more neglect and remain dry longer, especially after the plants have become well established. However, any protracted period of dryness will kill the plants. Periodic, light sprinkling as is described in greater detail earlier is best. When departing for a long summer vacation, simply relocate the containers to a protected, shaded area to preserve moisture.

Water the plants thoroughly once as winter approaches, so that they will not be too dry during the next several months; but check for the proper flow of water through the drainage material. Pooling moisture means certain death to alpine plants during their dormant period. Protect them against direct winter sun with a cover of pine branches. Shading and protection from moisture-reducing winds can be done by sticking small, conifer twigs into the ground around the plants.

As noted in the discussion on fertilization, after some time the supply of plant nutrients in the planting medium will be used up. While Basic Mix A contains an adequate supply of trace minerals to last for some time, the basic nutrients are used up more quickly in a small container. After the first year, liquid fertilizer should be applied in spring. Dissolve 1–2 grams of a water-soluble complete fertilizer in 1 quart (1 liter) of water. Apply fertilizer on a regular schedule of 2–3 week interludes during the spring. Stop fertilizing after mid-June, so the plants have an opportunity to mature and harden to survive the hardships of winter.

A planter created in the alpine style.

Selection of Plants

Criteria and Advice on Sources

The number of alpine and montane plants is so great that the novice may find it confusing to select those best suited to his purpose and needs. To help in this situation, the selection guides following the plant descriptions were created specifically for the beginner. The plants listed should assist the novice in getting started, but should also encourage his independent, creative involvement in selecting plants for his miniature garden.

Even before the important selection criteria of "purpose" and "location" are mentioned, it is useful to ask the question: What type of miniature garden do I wish to create? As already noted, particular species of small shrubs and dwarf trees are not suitable for some types of miniature gardens such as rockeries, slab gardens, wall gardens, or raised beds. Such species would quickly outgrow their intended place in the design. The type of garden also limits the use of other forms of plants: perennials, etc. The best, but by no means immutable, law of style is that rock gardens, slab gardens, wall gardens, and raised beds as well as perforated limestone structures demand alpine plants, while miniature rock gardens are best suited to a broader approach, using plants better noted for their display of flowers. This is particularly the case when using troughs, boxes, planters, and other containers. The decision needs to be firmly fixed, since decorative plantings use different species than do the alpine forms—not to mention special collections formed by ardent collectors. The latter is given equal billing in this book, since I distinguish between rock garden shrubs and alpine plants. Let us not forget, though, that this difference is not so great that the two can never be harmoniously combined. The collector should also remain open-minded about new introductions which enlarge the selection of plants. Newly introduced species from the wild garden by hybrids and selected sports are worthy of equal attention. Some plant lovers insist that only the true wild species should be included in their collections. The rigid pursuit of such an orthodox position will deny the collector much of the wealth and beauty of the flowering alpine plant world. Many species native to high elevations—whose color intensity and floriferous habit can be so exciting and satisfying—grow poorly when transferred to a garden. Only through selection of free-flowering and vigorous forms, or through hybridizing of the best forms, can these plants be successfully introduced into the garden. For example, *Silene acaulis*—covered with flowers in the mountains—is only a verdant, compact pillow with one or two flowers in the

71

garden. On the other hand, its cultivated form *S. acaulis* 'Floribunda' is covered with red flowers even in the lowlands.

It is imperative to solicit and then study the catalogs of nurseries and garden centers. The novice, in particular, will find quite a sufficient selection from these sources. Rare species suitable for the advanced grower and collector can often be obtained from specialty alpine nurseries.

Knowledge grows and many problems solved through conversation with fellow gardeners or the advice of experts from specialty nurseries or botanical gardens. More useful are the books dealing with alpine plants, several of which are listed in the bibliography and are highly recommended.

Anyone growing alpine or mountain plants will benefit from membership in the plant societies formed to serve such gardeners (see Appendix). These are all very active organizations conducting sizable seed exchanges every year and publishing first-rate journals on dwarf trees, shrubs, rock garden, and alpine plants. They also maintain lists of available seeds that are a real treasure trove for collectors of alpine plants.

Description of Species and Varieties

The following selection of plants does not pretend to be a complete compilation, nor does it aim to be a comprehensive overview. It is my intention only to present a relatively wide selection of reliable plants from which the reader may choose those best suited to his design needs. The list also contains a number of rarer plants for miniature gardens and is sufficiently wide-ranging to permit personal taste and aims to play the principal role in the final decision.

(*23*) Troughs look particularly attractive when placed in front of a peaceful backdrop, here a Hornbeam hedge and beside a flagstone path. Both troughs feature hanging plants—in the first, primarily juniper, *Juniperus horizontalis* 'Glauca', and on the right *Onosma albo-roseum*. At the foot of the troughs are drifts of *Sagina subulata*. (*24*) *Sempervivum* 'Othello' between rocks and next to a dwarf juniper, *J. squamata* 'Blue Star.' (*25*) *Geranium subcaulescens* 'Splendens'. This rock geranium is valuable in the alpine garden for it flowers for some weeks and is brightly colored.

73

Dwarf Conifers

I repeat my earlier warning to avoid selecting species/cultivars that grow too large for a specific site. Where no other cultural advice is given, the plants will thrive in Basic Mix A.

Abies (Fir)
Of the deep green balsam firs from the White Mountains in North America, the dwarf form *A. balsamea* 'Nana' is best suited for miniature alpine gardens. It grows slowly and has a compact, round shape with beautiful dark green needles. The dwarf form of the White Fir, *A. concolor* 'Compacta', has needles with a bluish tinge and irregular, dense growth. In time, it may become too large for an alpine miniature garden; however, it is well suited for troughs and planters. Another species suited for trough culture is the dwarf sport of *A. koreana*, known as 'Compact Dwarf'; it is a slow-growing plant and bears dark green needles. *Abies lasiocarpa* var. *arizonica* is a low-growing alpine fir which is also a good trough garden plant, especially since it grows quite slowly when immature. It is cone-shaped and has needles with a blue tinge. Be sure to remove the center shoot in order to maintain its attractive dwarf habit.

Cedrus (Cedar)
Among the numerous cedar species, there is scarcely a single type that is truly dwarf in habit and so suited for an alpine miniature garden. There is an alternative, though, for the trough garden. Select either the slow, compact Cyprus Cedar, *C. brevifolia*, or the slow-growing dwarf form of the Cedar of Lebanon, *C. libani*

'Sargenti'. Be sure to trim and prune Cyprus Cedar from the beginning to maintain the dwarf habit. For a trough garden, use plants propagated from branch cuttings if at all possible. Hybrids tend to grow taller, while plants from cuttings, when planted along the edge of the trough, will tend to trail downward.

Chamaecyparis (False Cypress)
Many False Cypress cultivars are perfect for planting into containers or even large troughs, thanks to their low habit. I shall mention just a few from the sizable selection available. Without doubt, the most attractive is the well-known and widely grown *C. obtusa* 'Nana Gracilis', the Japanese False Cypress. It grows slowly, has a compact, conical habit and shell-like branching. It can be maintained in a diminutive state through judicious pruning. *Chamaecyparis pisifera* 'Plumosa Compressa', is a slowly-growing, dwarf cultivar with a compact habit and irregular, bell-shaped appearance. The needles tend to be yellowish green. Unfortunately, this form is easily damaged by bright, direct sunlight; the resulting scattered, browned areas can be prevented by placing the plant in an area with indirect light. If a more columnar appearance is desired, use the fine-needled, blue *C. lawsoniana* 'Ellwoodii Pygmy' in a trough or even in a window box. Be aware, though, that this plant dislikes drought and prefers light shade. A golden yellow pyramid is provided by *C. lawsoniana* 'Minima Aurea', while the cone of *C. thyoides* is more gradual. Both grow slowly and are suited for trough culture, in which the latter variety grows even more dwarf.

Cryptomeria (Japanese Cedar)

Japanese Cedar, *C. japonica*, prefers moist soil for good growth and should be protected from direct winter sun, which is the reason for planting the varieties best suited for our purposes in a shaded trough or in wet locations. A true dwarf is 'Vilminiana' with a very compact, low and bushy habit. In winter the plant turns brilliantly reddish brown and then greens again in spring. 'Globosa Nana' grows short, compact and fluffy, and bears gray-green summer foliage. Both cultivars do well in the alpine miniature garden. The taller, usually only creeping, varieties should be used for trough and container gardening where they can be kept compact more easily. They also benefit from partial shade. 'Bandaisugi', an irregular, compact but upright plant, and the cone-shaped 'Cristata' are also slow growers. 'Kilmacurragh' has an irregular, compact, and ovoid habit and is very picturesque.

Ginkgo

Although ginkgos reach considerable height in the open, they are also well suited for container culture. The Ginkgo (*G. biloba*), an ancient species, has an interesting leaf form and is deciduous. In Japan it is a popular bonsai plant. With appropriate training, it can also be maintained in a trough garden as a dwarf tree.

Juniperus (Juniper)

Together with the pines, juniper species provide the basic structure for the evergreen appearance of alpine miniature gardens. One of the best dwarf forms for troughs, slab gardens, rock gardens and raised beds is *J. communis* 'Compressa'. This very slow-growing dwarf, columnar juniper with its dense, narrow growth is an impressive jewel in any miniature garden or trough. Singly or planted in groups, it gives alpine gardens that extra touch. The "flaw" noticed in winter, when several shoots turn brown, cannot be held against this dwarf variety. Four varieties of *J. squamata* are available; the best of the lot is the intense blue, low-growing 'Blue Star' which has a dense, ball-shaped appearance. Older, less-dense examples of this cultivar have a lovely and picturesque appearance similar to Japanese bonsai. The striking blue color of 'Blue Star' cannot be duplicated with the flat-growing 'Blue Carpet' or 'Loderi', a blue-gray, low, dense, dwarf form with an upright, somewhat columnar habit. The low-growing variety 'Pygmaea' is also not up to these standards.

The best low-growing, dwarf juniper is *J. horizontalis* 'Glauca'. This blue juniper creeps along the ground, hangs over the edge of a trough, or spreads between the rocks in an alpine rock garden. The plant can be pruned without fear, should it become too vigorous. *Juniperus chinensis* 'Blaauw's Varietät', suited for troughs as well as windowboxes, has a very dense, irregular and upright habit; its color tends toward blue-green. More yellowish in color is the slow-growing *J. communis* 'Depressa Aurea', which is also a dense, flat, spreading variety.

Larix (Larch)

Although Larch can reach an impressive height, the Japanese often use the species *L. kaempferi* (syn. *L. leptolepis*) as a bonsai specimen. It can be kept in a dwarf state in troughs or a large planter. The same can be said for the trailing variety 'Pendula', which does not grow quite as vigorously.

Picea (Spruce)

Low-growing spruce are numerous, and among them are several true, dwarf plants. Almost all compact and low-growing varieties are suited for planting in troughs and can be maintained as dwarves very well. *Picea glauca* 'Laurin' is an exceptional slow dwarf. This cultivar—developed after World War II—reaches a height of only 8–12 in. (20–30cm) in 10–15 years; with a growth of only ¾ in. per year, it is easily one of the best dwarf trees in the alpine miniature garden. Its growth is dense, and the regular, perfectly conical shape gives the appearance of having been created through topiary. A broad, oval counterpoint is *P. glauca* 'Echiniformis'. Due to its dense and pillow-shaped form and bluish color, this true dwarf is an exceptional choice for the alpine miniature garden. The slow-growing dwarf *Picea abies* 'Echiniformis' is characterized by green foliage, very dense growth, and an irregular rounded appearance. *P. abies* 'Gregoryana' is a close twin with somewhat shorter needles. Very attractive needles are found in the low-growing dwarf version of *P. glauca* 'Alberta Globe'. This one also grows slowly and remains low and globular.

Not as perfectly ball-shaped but spreading and rounded-off is the dwarf version of *P. mariana* 'Nana'. Its irregular, low and slow growth endears this blue-gray spruce cultivar to lovers of miniature rock gardens, troughs, and slab gardens. The Colorado Blue Spruce, *P. pungens* 'Glauca Globosa', is a dwarf variety with beautiful blue needles. In time this plant will grow too large for the site, and so is recommended primarily for trough or container gardening. Nevertheless, its habit can best be described as dense and low-growing. Dainty, fresh green needles are found on the dwarf form of the Caucasian Spruce, *P. orientalis* 'Gracilis'. If this plant is to reach its potential and develop the characteristic com-

(26) Trough made of sandstone, standing next to a shrub hedge and planted with hardy varieties: *Thymus praecox* var. *pseudolanuginosus* (Thyme) spreads beyond the edge; next to that in a blue-gray pillow *Dianthus gratianopolitanus* (Cheddar Pink), and also several sempervivums and rosettes of *Saxifraga* varieties. (27) Beautiful flower head of the saxifrage *S. cotyledon* 'Southside Seedling'. At the onset of flowering, the individual blossoms turn red at their bases. (28) Blooming *Saxifraga longifolia*. Unfortunately, this variety of *Saxifraga* dies after blooming. Culture can be continued only with new seedlings.

pact growth, do not over-fertilize it in trough gardens. There is also a good dwarf cultivar of *P. omorika*, 'Nana'. Its dense, upright appearance is well suited for larger troughs. The cultivar *P. omorika* 'Frohnleiten', on the other hand, has no center shoot so grows irregularly. Especially picturesque in a larger trough is *P. abies* 'Inversa', a trailing spruce with pendulous branches.

Pinus (Pine)

In addition to the dwarf spruces and junipers, the dwarf pines are exceptional plants for the creation of alpine miniature gardens. They often develop particularly bizarre forms in the mountains, and are able to thrive despite the harsh weather of higher elevations. There are low-growing pine cultivars, but only a few are truly slow-growing and dwarf in habit. That is why dwarf pines especially need to be pruned and disbranched regularly in order to preserve the plants' small, low habit.

The typical dwarf form of the Mountain Pine, *P. mugo* ssp. *pumilio*, remains very low, but in time spreads considerably so has to be pruned back periodically. A very slow-growing, true dwarf with rounded features is the deep green *P. mugo* 'Mops'. With these characteristics, it is suited for all types of miniature gardens. However, in troughs it develops especially well into a perfect, dwarf grower. Other noteworthy cultivars of *P. mugo* are 'Humpy' and 'Slavinii'; both are truly tiny and remain so, but they are difficult to find. 'Humpy' develops gradually into an irregularly-shaped bush, while 'Slavinii' grows very densely and compactly. In the last several years, the very pretty dwarf form *P.*

sylvestris 'Perkeo' has been developed from what used to be a very ugly pine. This one also grows low and has a bushy, dense appearance. Another very good and slow-growing dwarf cultivar is *P. sylvestris* 'Beauvronensis'.

Most of the low-growing, but not true dwarf, pine forms are not appropriate for alpine miniature gardens. At the same time they are so interesting that they are hard to resist. If one takes extra effort to keep these cultivars in bounds by careful feeding and pruning, they will make quite picturesque forms in a trough garden, a larger planter, or even in a window box.

Pinus pumila, a dwarf, creeping pine, remains low-growing but at the same time can become too expansive for miniature gardens. However, in a trough this variety is outstanding, especially its blue, dwarf cultivar 'Glauca'. This one grows much like a Japanese bonsai in trough gardens. *Pinus leucodermis* 'Compact Gem', another dwarf, possesses dark green needles and a stout appearance and grows slowly. The dwarf form of Eastern White Pine, *P. strobus* 'Nana', has long, soft, and gray-blue foliage, and also grows slowly into a stout and dense plant. *Pinus cembra* 'Nana' can be kept small only in a trough garden or other container. It is a slow and very dense-growing variety of the Arolla Pine alpine. *Pinus cembra* 'Pygmaea' possesses irregular, low growth habits with no center growing tip. Of the Japanese Red Pines, *P. densiflora* 'Umbraculifera' is well suited for trough culture where it presents a lovely appearance with its umbrellalike, flat habit. *Pinus parviflora* 'Glauca' is popular in Japan among bonsai growers. If it is planted in a trough or even a window box, it can be kept in a dwarf state. The cultivar grows slowly, upright, and never spreads; consequently, it can also be recommended for use in medium-sized alpine miniature gardens.

Pseudotsuga

The dwarf Douglas Fir, *P. menziesii* 'Fletcheri', is a slow-growing, dwarf form with blue-green needles and a somewhat spreading habit. It is suited for planting in a trough garden.

Taxus (Yew)

Yews do not like hot weather or dry conditions, making them good for shaded, somewhat more moist locations. All species withstand severe pruning well, which is the method used to keep even vigorous forms in check.

The slowest-growing yew is *T. cuspidata* 'Nana', noted for its low, dense and irregular appearance. With its dark green foliage and picturesque stout trunk, this cultivar fits alpine miniature gardens or trough gardens well. The slow-growing English Yew, *Taxus baccata* 'Fastigiata', presents a narrow, columnar appearance; the tip shoots can be trimmed back periodically to keep the plant in the dwarf state. *T. baccata* 'Fastigiata Aurea' has golden yellow shoots. In other respects, this columnar variety possesses the same growth characteristics as the dark green yews.

Thuja (Arborvitae)

Of the many different kinds of *Thuja*, two cultivars of *T. orientalis* stand out as being excellent plants for miniature gardens and troughs. Both are slow growers and have a dense habit. The yellowish green 'Aurea Nana' has an evenly oval and well-trained appearance. 'Rosedalis Compacta', on the other hand, presents a softer, more irregular shape. This gorgeous, dwarf plant glows golden during bud-break in spring, then turns green during summer, and in winter changes to purple.

Thujopsis (Hiba Cedar)

The dwarf form of the Hiba Cedar, *T. dolabrata* 'Nana', should be planted where there is sufficient moisture and some shade. It grows close to the ground with scalelike, bright green needles and finely divided branches.

Tsuga (Hemlock)

Hemlock also prefers shadier places and so benefits from a location in a trough with partial shade. *Tsuga canadensis* 'Nana' is a low-growing, pillow-shaped dwarf with a fresh green appearance. *Tsuga canadensis* 'Jeddeloh' is much easier to grow; its growth pattern is much like 'Nana' but presents a round form with a funnel-shaped center. *Tsuga canadensis* 'Pendula' is a lovely form with pendulous branches and very dense habit.

Dwarf Deciduous Trees

The truly small and dwarf varieties of deciduous trees and shrubs are almost all blessed with interesting branch patterns and superb flowers. We cannot do without them in alpine miniature gardens. Almost all fare well in Basic Mix A; I have noted any exceptions in their respective descriptions. Those which have the habit of semishrubs are not included here as I will deal with them in detail in the section devoted to rock garden perennials and alpine plants. Azaleas, dwarf rhododendrons, and several bog plants with similar soil needs are discussed in a single entry.

Acer (Maple)

Of the many maple species and cultivars, only the slow-growing Golden Fullmoon Maple, *A. japonicum* 'Aureum', can be counted upon to remain small in alpine troughs. This form is renowned for its golden yellow foliage and intriguing habit.

Cotoneaster (Cotoneaster)

The several low, evergreen forms of cotoneaster cannot be omitted from any list of favorite alpine garden genera. Covered in spring with white or light pink flowers, and balanced in fall with thick stands of red berries, they must have a place in any miniature garden. Planted at the edge of a trough or slab garden, cotoneaster hugs the rock and spreads over the edge. The slow-growing cultivar *C. dammeri* 'Streibs Findling' is well suited for such a situation. It enjoys following the rock face, has small, evergreen leaves, and displays relatively large flowers during spring. Similar to it—and also very floriferous—is the Himalayan *C. congestus*. During autumn, this cotoneaster is covered with bright red berries. The well-known, large-leaved, spreading species *C. dammeri* recently produced the cultivar 'Pforzheim', a very dense and low-growing sport. It is well suited for the purpose of forming evergreen mats in alpine miniature gardens.

(*29*) *Delosperma cooperi*, the Trailing Ice Plant, responds to attentive care by producing numerous flowers. (*30*) *Acantholimon graminifolium* is ideal for throughs in full sun. (*31*) Glacier Ranunculus, *R. glacialis*, thrives in narrow crevices and on gravelly soil. (*32*) The long-stemmed blooms of *Edraianthus tenuifolius* prefer the support of a rockface. (*33*) Protect *Lewisia cotyledon* 'Sunset Strain' from winter moisture! (*34*) Rock Dianthus are a lovely, decorative accent for any rock garden. The large flowers of *D. gracilis* rise over dense pillows of foliage.

Cytisus (Broom)

The name "broom" is also used for the genus *Genista*, creating much nomenclatural confusion. *Cytisus* offers, in the form of the dwarf brooms, true treasures for the alpine miniature garden. The lowest species, which truly hugs the ground as it spreads, is *C. decumbens*. No gardener should miss the mass of golden yellow blooms during May and June. *Cytisus ardoini*, a dwarf broom from Europe, does not spread quite so expansively; the habit is somewhat upright, and the entire plant remains compact. Its blooms are much like those of *C. decumbens*, appearing at the same time as well. For trough culture also consider *C. kewensis*, the Kew Broom. It has a dwarf, bushy habit, and the pendulous branches are covered in April and May with light yellow flowers.

Daphne (Daphne)

The alpine forms of Common Daphne are jewels in any alpine collection. When the mostly pink-red blooms exude their superb fragrance every May, the heart of any lover of alpine plants must beat a bit faster. All alpine *Daphne* require a supplement of coarse rock to Basic Mix A, and they need superb drainage. Perlite or fine pumice must be added to the planting medium to coarsen and lighten the soil.

An entire series of useful cultivars have been derived from the Garland Daphne, *D. cneorum*, native to the Alps, and all should be considered by the collector and grower. The beginner should focus on both *D. cneorum* and its more robust-growing sport 'Major'. This *Daphne* is both low-growing and dense, and in May is covered with pink, fragrant flowers.

Daphne arbuscula from Czechoslovakia's Tatra Mountains is also low-growing. The dark green, dense foliage pillow is decorated with pink-lavender flowers in May and June.

Bushier and more compact, but evergreen and low-growing, are *D. sericea* with carmine-pink flowers and *D. collina* with more purely pink ones. *Daphne napolitana* also has a bushy habit and deep purple-pink blossoms; the slow-growing *D. glandulosa* blooms carmine-pink and is also low in stature, as is *D. oleoides*.

The collector can choose from an entire series of dwarf forms. All grow well in airy soil of the type I have denoted as Basic Mix A. Exclusively, rock plants like *D. petraea* should be planted in Basic Mix B, amended by a goodly amount of perlite or pumice.

Erica (Heather)

Erica herbacea (syn. *E. carnea*), as Alpine Heath is also known, should not be left out of any alpine rock garden. Its early bloom is a sure messenger of spring in late winter. As long as it is planted in aerated soil with the addition of leafmold, it will grow just about anywhere. *Erica* is sensitive to soggy conditions during winter, though, which is usually the reason it often fails in window boxes or trough gardens.

There are many cultivars of *E. herbacea*. The best known among them is the early-blooming 'Winter Beauty' with intensely reddish pink blooms. Blooming somewhat later, 'Vivelli' has beautiful, dark carmine-red flowers and dark foliage, but it is a weaker grower. Other cultivars are also useful, particularly the white-flowering 'Springwood'.

Genista (Broom)

The name "broom" is also used for the genus *Cytisus*, which leads to the confusion usual with common names. The smallest species is *G. villarsii* with golden yellow blossoms; since it grows only slowly, it remains small. That is the reason for setting it in the tighter sites—the edge of a trough or between the rocks in a rock garden. They also fare well in hollows in perforated limestone.

The dwarf form *G. sagittalis* var. *minor* (syn. *G. delphinensis*) has dwarfish, creeping features and can also be recommended. The Sand Broom, which tends to spread too quickly to be useful for miniature gardens, has a more suitable dwarf form, *G. pilosa* 'Nana'. It forms flat, dense pillows decorated in May with golden yellow blooms. Of the more vigorous species, several are suitable for trough culture: *G. lydia*, a golden yellow dwarf broom, blooms later than most species and is pendulous and rotund; *G. radiata* grows low to the ground and looks spikey, while *G. horrida* is denser, thorny, and ball-shaped in appearance. All of these brooms grow well in Basic Mix A when planted in a sunny location and, once acclimated, can tolerate dry conditions.

Salix (Willow)

Many forms of dwarf willow are very effective in a rock garden; however, when planted in alpine miniature gardens, they quickly grow too large and destroy the harmony of the scene. A true dwarf is *S. serpyllifolia* which forms a green carpet, its dense foliage covered with tiny, roundish leaves. Just as useful is *S. reticulata*, an alpine willow. It is also a creeper and can cover an entire boulder with its impressive large foliage. *Salix retusa* spreads its branches farther afield, but it also likes to hug the rocks. At the other extreme, *S. × simulatrix* grows too openly. This dwarf willow from the Swiss Engadin Valley is best planted in a trough garden, where its pendulous branches can droop over the edge. Almost all other species grow bushier and have an upright habit. As pretty as the impression might be, they are just too vigorous for an alpine miniature garden.

Sorbus (Mountain Ash)

The Dwarf Mountain Ash, *S. reducta*, is a truly slow-growing dwarf species with a dense, bushy habit and large, white blossoms. In autumn, numbers of dark pink berries appear. This ash is rare and best left to collectors seeking the unusual.

Ulmus (Elm)

Among the elms one can find dwarf cultivars suitable for alpine gardens. The most notable is *U. elegantissima* 'Jacqueline Hillier', distinguished by very slow growth, low habit, and interesting conformation. It can also be trained very easily as a bonsai plant.

Rhododendron (Rhododendron, Azalea)

Novices are frequently confused when the terms rhododendron and azalea are mentioned in the same breath. Botanically, though, the proper term for both plants is *Rhododendron*. Azaleas are merely a subgroup of *Rhododendron*.

Rhododendron belong to the so-called humus-loving or wetland plants, and consequently they have to be treated and planted differently from all the plants discussed thus far. Generally, they prefer a location in partial to full shade and fresh, moist soil. Basic Mix D is preferred by these plants, since it adds perlite or fine pumice to the topsoil and makes it especially light and water-permeable.

The gardener is encouraged to try *R. hirsutum* and *R. ferrugineum* in alpine miniature gardens. Avoid following the adage that rhododendron species native to limestone mountains do well in an alkaline soil. In such mountains, rhododendron usually grow in locations with a considerable layer of humus, so that the plants hardly come in contact with the underlying limestone soil. If they can be assured of a humus-enriched, light, and well-aerated soil, they thrive in regions with alkaline soils. In alpine miniature gardens based on Basic Mix A, but in which the sites for rhododendron have been filled with Basic Mix D, there should be little difficulty in raising these plants. Surround rootballs at planting time with an inch or so of wet peat all around, to encourage root hair development. Rhododendron flourish in shady locations, so makes a great contribution to such areas in the miniature garden. The surface around rhododendrons should be covered with a mulch of 1-in.-deep (2.5 cm) peat.

The most impressive rhododendron cultivars were developed from *R. multiflorum*. All are floriferous, low-growing, bushy plants covered with flowers during May. These Japanese dwarf rhododendron are known under the appellation of *R. multiflorum* hybrids and are offered in nursery catalogs under such a name or simply as some form of *Azalea*.

There are any number of color types, all of which are better in the garden than the somewhat tender *Azalea* species which also bloom poorly. The gardener is urged to survey the many *Azalea* cultivars suitable for this climate and then make selections based on design considerations.

Aside from these Japanese dwarf rhododendrons, which provide a sparkling display every spring in the alpine miniature garden or garden trough, there are several other species and cultivars well suited for our purposes. The very low-growing, blue *R. impeditum* usually flowers in April. There is also a large-flowered, dark purple sport with a beautiful, dense evergreen habit and somewhat shiny leaves; *R. multiflorum* 'Moerheimii' is a pretty, very low-growing and dense rhododendron with small leaves and lilac-pink blossoms. This May-blooming variety is a good choice for trough gardens with shade. The same can be said for the somewhat poorer-blooming low Tibetan rhododendron *R. keleticum*, which bears purple-carmine-pink flowers. Very low-growing, dense, and rather spreading is the evergreen *R. radicans*. However, it produces few flowers and even they need some encouragement to open. One of the *R. repens* hybrids is particularly effective at the edge of an alpine rock garden.

The so-called dwarf rhododendron of the Alps, *Rhodothamnus chamaecistus*, is primarily a plant for the collector. It should be planted in light shade in Basic Mix B, amended with a considerable amount of perlite or crushed rock, such as pumice. Another plant of interest primarily to expert growers is *Loiseleuria procumbens*. Its habit is creeping and mat-forming, and its upright flowers appear in May. In a porous soil made of Basic Mix D, perlite, sand, or pumice and in semishade, this species fares quite well.

Between azaleas and dwarf rhododendrons, *Gaultheria procumbens* makes a good groundcover. It needs a soil and location similar to those of the rhododendrons. The plant creates a solid, low mat with evergreen, shiny leaves; in autumn it is covered with red berries.

Rock Garden Flowering Perennials

The following selection contains species and cultivars with a proven record for permanent and striking planting in window boxes, terrace planters, and vessels, including troughs and slab gardens. As noted earlier, a great number of other winter-hardy perennials can also be used, so this listing should be viewed as one of dependable plants with which to get started. When combined with dwarf conifers or dwarf deciduous trees and shrubs, a very attractive garden can be made. Basic Mix A is the soil to be used in every case.

Acaena (Sheep Bur)
Sheep Bur is the common name given these robust, very low-growing, matting subshrubs from New Zealand. When planted at the edge of a trough they soon drape over it. The decorative, somewhat prickly burrs are borne above the dense, evergreen pillows. They are also useful for plantings at the edge of an alpine rock garden, where they may form larger mats. I recommend *A. buchananii* with its light brown foliage and the somewhat more delicate-looking *A. microphylla.*

Alyssum
Powerful yellow splashes of color are the springtime contribution of the well-known *A. saxatile* cultivars, also known as robust plants. 'Compactum' remains low-growing; the double blooms of 'Plenum' are golden yellow, but colors can range from the orange-yellow 'Dudley Neville' to the light yellow of 'Citrinum'. *Alyssum montanum* 'Berggold' forms a low, ash-gray cushion. With its bright yellow flowers, the plant fits in well at the edge of a trough next to *Aubrieta.*

Androsace (Rock Jasmine)
Most species of *Androsace* belong in true alpine gardens. *Androsace primuloides* from the Himalayas can also be used simply as a flowering plant. With runners on the soil surface, it creates dense, rosette pillows covered in May with reddish pink flowers.

Antennaria
Antennaria diocia var. *borealis* (syn. *A. tomentosa* hort.) develops very low, dense, and whitish-leaved carpets which are well suited for the ornamental trough or slab garden. The form 'Rubra' possesses red flower heads and foliage which is less hirsute and white. 'Nywood' is noted for its beautiful, pink flowers.

Arabis (Rockcress)
The white-flowering *A. caucasica* 'Schneehaube' makes a fine show between the rocks or at the edge of larger troughs, slab gardens, or window boxes. Its tight, evergreen pillows trail far down the side of containers and—together with *Aubrieta*, Moss Pink and *Alyssum*—create a colorful scene in the spring. The double *A. caucasica* 'Plena' is another fine cultivar.

Armeria (Thrift)
The bright purple-pink, ball-shaped flowers of *A. maritima* rise in May above the dense, grassy foliage cushion. If after

two or three years the plant has spread too extensively, divide and replant.

Aster

The tenacious Alpine Aster, *A. alpinus*, bears blue flowers on short stems which vary in color intensity, depending upon the cultivar. All the cultivars are worthwhile. If flowers are needed late in the year, plant the autumn-blooming, low-growing *A. dumosus*, particularly the lowest, dark pink form.

Aubrieta

Those gardeners who take the care to check on the better *Aubrieta* varieties will be rewarded in spring with a mass of splendid color in troughs, slab gardens, or even in window boxes. Seedlings are often offered at lower prices, but they produce neither the large flower, nor color, nor the richness of bloom, nor the longer duration of bloom characteristic of named varieties propagated vegetatively.

The hybridizers have created so many fine cultivars that the gardener willing to investigate their entire range will find a super abundance of plants for any design objective.

Campanula (Bellflower)

The summer-flowering Bellflower has become a permanent fixture in flowering miniature gardens with some light shade. Again, any number of splendid, low-growing cultivars of very compact *C. carpatica* are available to the gardener willing to search them out! The same is true of the cultivars of the robust *C. poscharskyana*. From June through August, these cultivars bloom in great abundance if set in a relatively moist location.

Carlina (Silver Thistle)

In a larger trough, placed between dwarf conifers, *C. acaulis* makes a fine appearance when its large, silver-white blooms open in autumn. After flowering, the seed head remains attractive well into the winter.

Cerastium (Snow-In-Summer)

The vigorously growing *Cerastium*, so popular in the garden as a groundcover, is also a useful plant for the same purpose in large trough gardens or even window boxes. It is attractive when combined with *Aubrieta*, Moss Pink, and other cushion-

(35) *Aethionema warleyense* (Stonecress) requires a site in well-drained soil and between rocks. (36) Skillful gardeners can coax beautiful blooms even in the garden from *Leontopodium alpinum* (Edelweiss). (37) Perforated limestone is the right choice for *Edraianthus graminiflorus*. (38) *Saxifraga oppositifolia* 'Splendens' prefers granular soil and some shade. (39) *Gentiana acaulis* 'Dinarica', an example of the stemless gentian, prefers a site between rocks. (40) *Edraianthus dinaricus* is a jewel for planting in perforated limestone boulders.

forming plants. *Cerastium tomentosum* var. *columnae*, with its hairy, white cushion and pure white blossoms, is one of the best varieties, since it does not grow as rapidly as the species.

Chrysogonum

Chrysogonum virginianum is a lovely plant which is decorated from July until September with golden yellow flowers arising from low, leafy cushions. The long duration of bloom makes this plant particularly sought-after.

Dianthus (Pink)

Apart from the spring-flowering, cushion-forming plants, the Cheddar Pink, *D. gratianopolitanus* (formerly *D. caesius*), is essential for any miniature garden. Above the very dense, usually bluish gray pillows (which look attractive year-round) the large pink and red flowers appear between May and mid-summer. There are many cultivars with good color. The best-growing are found in the catalogs of perennial nurseries; these Pinks are heavy-flowering and have remarkably large flowers. *Dianthus all-woodi*, a similarly vigorously growing species, has a somewhat more delicately tinted flower with a solid colored throat.

Euphorbia (Spurge)

The long, scalelike shoots of *E. myrsinites* seem to be tailormade for use in trough gardens, where the plant provides a picturesque backdrop, or at the edge of a slab garden or window box, where it can trail over the side.

Gentiana (Gentian)

Of this typical alpine wildflower, two varieties are especially useful for flower display: *G. septemfida* var. *lagodechiana* largely grows without requiring special attention, remains low, and displays blue flowers in late summer. Famous for its intense blue is the Stemless Gentian of the Alps, *G. acaulis*; the selected cultivar 'Dinarica' is a heavy bloomer with large flowers, and for this reason is preferred.

Gypsophila (Baby's Breath)

Gypsophila repens has several low-growing cultivars with double flowers, which open *en masse* during summer to provide a stunning display. This form of Baby's Breath is also well suited for planting in window boxes or among dwarf conifers.

Helianthemum (Sunrose)

In early summer, the low-growing Sunroses knit dense-blooming carpets that drape over the edge of a trough or window box. But only the single-flowering, dwarf, creeping forms are usable since they are among the more frost-resistant. The hybrid 'Sterntaler' creates beautifully dense pillows and has golden yellow flowers. The flowers of *H. nummularium* (syn. *H. chamaecistus*) 'Zonatus' possess red throats and bright green, leafy foliage in cushion form.

Heliosperma see Silene

Iberis (Candytuft)

Aside from the very well-known, compact species *I. sempervirens*, covered in spring with large, white flowers, the low-growing, cushion-forming *I. saxatilis* is a good choice for ornamental plantings. This species tends to bloom again in autumn.

Inula

The dwarf *Inula, I. ensifolia* 'Compacta', is a richly flowering plant with diminutive growth habits, a bushy structure, and golden yellow flowers during summer.

Minuartia

Absolutely necessary for planting window boxes, troughs, or slab gardens is the white-flowering *M. laricifolia*. Draped over rocks or the edge of a miniature garden, the dense cushions of this durable, trouble-free plant have a graceful appearance.

Oenothera (Evening Primrose)

Large, golden flowers decorate the Evening Primrose, *O. missouriensis*, from late summer well into autumn. Its low, creeping habit assigns this plant to the edge of the trough. While it is not evergreen, its cushion form, late flowering period and over-sized, funnel-shaped flowers more than make up for it. The Evening Primrose is highly recommended.

Phlox

Moss Pink (*P. subulata*) is a very popular cushion-forming plant found in nearly everyone's garden, and it is well-suited for miniature gardens. In spring the dense, green cushions practically disappear under the abundant flowers. Together with *Aubrieta* and Candytuft, Moss Pink grows over the edge of window boxes, troughs, and slab gardens and hugs the base of rocks in alpine gardens. The recommended cultivars are: 'Atropurpurea', dark carmine-red; 'Daisy Hill', salmon; 'G. F. Wilson', slate-blue and very vigorous; 'Leuchtstern', dark pink with a very solid cushion; and 'Temiskaming', bright purple.

Potentilla (Cinquefoil)

The bright golden flowers of *P. aurea* appear on top of low, dense mats. The cultivar 'Goldklumpen' is particularly floriferous. Not quite as flat-growing, but just as heavy-blooming, is *P. aurea* ssp. *chrysocraspeda* (syn. *P. ternata*); its golden yellow flowers are somewhat darker in hue than those of the former.

Saponaria (Soapwort)

The mats of *S. ocymoides* trail well down the sides of a trough or a planter. This plant is a perfect choice to span the flowering interval between spring and summer with its load of reddish pink blooms, which appear in early summer.

Saxifraga (Saxifrage)

True treasures for alpine displays are the different Saxifrage species. Several can be warmly recommended for permanent ornamental garden uses. While the rosette-forming Saxifrage species prefer to be planted among rocks, the mossy species create green carpets, especially in shaded locations. The *S. arendsii* hybrids are the best-known species of this type: 'Blutenteppich' has carmine-pink flowers; 'Triumph' shows off dark ruby-red flowers. Dense, low, mossylike cushions which turn bronze during winter are the characteristics of the white-flowering *S. hypnoides* var. *egemmulosa* (syn. *S. kingii*). Another, *S. muscoides* 'Findling', flowers profusely, with the white flowers obscuring the dense dark-green foliage carpet.

Sedum (Stonecrop)

Many *Sedum* species are easily cultivated spreading plants in gardens and rock gardens. Thanks to their hardiness they are also enormously useful in miniature gardens. Of exceptional value is *S. floriferum* 'Weihenstephaner Gold' with its dense foliage and golden flowers. *Sedum kamtschaticum* 'Fol. Var.' is effective as well; its pretty leaf structure is edged in gold. *Sedum spurium* 'Coccineum' has reddish leaves and lilac-red flowers. In autumn, the purplish flowers of *S. cauticolum* rise above the blue-tinged leaves.

Sempervivum (Houseleek)

The houseleek species are most attractive when grown among rocks in an alpine garden. Moreover, there are many cultivars even more suitable for use in a flowering setting, particularly those with sizable leaf rosettes. From the multitude of available cultivars, let me recommend several: 'Commander Hay' is distinguished by very large, rust-red rosettes edged in green; the flowers often attain a diameter of 8 in. (20cm) and are reddish pink. The purplish-red rosettes of the cultivar 'Sponnier' are just as large and have a wider, green edge. 'Amtmann Fischer' sports violet-purple rosettes with even darker colored tips and wine-red flowers. Large, rust-red rosettes edged in green are typical of 'Othello'; the flowers are dark pink. 'Purpurriese' also has dark pink flowers and distinctive purplish rosettes. Broad green rosettes with beautifully contrasting reddish leaf edges are the mark of 'Seerosenstern'. Somewhat smaller are the vibrant red rosettes edged in green of 'Maby II'. Beyond that, there are any number of other good species and cultivars with rosettes of every size. Several more are listed and described in the section on alpine plants.

(**41**) *Saxifraga longifolia* (Royal Saxifrage) has a striking, noble rosette. (**42**) *Geranium cinereum* 'Ballerina' flowers are especially abundant. (**43**) The native form of the American *Lewisia cotyledon* should be protected from too much moisture. (**44**) *Townsendia wilcoxiana,* from North America's Rocky Mountains, is very moisture sensitive. The flowers resemble those of the Alpine Aster. (**45**) *Anacyclus depressus* opens red buds to display white flowers. (**46**) *Artemisia stelleriana* (Dusty Miller) provides an effective contrast to the dark rock with its silver foliage.

91

The dense rosettes set off the attractive blooms of a *Sempervivum*.

Silene

Two attributes make *S. alpestris* (syn. *Heliosperma alpestre*) 'Pleniflorum' valuable for miniature gardens: its summer flowering period and the double, white blooms standing above a diminutive green cushion. It does well in both shaded and sunny locations. *Silene schafta* 'Splendens' is especially recommended for autumn flowering. It forms loose cushions, and its bright carmine-red blossoms appear in late summer and remain well into autumn.

Thymus (Thyme)

The summer-flowering *T. serpyllum* 'Coccineum' forms dense, low mats between which the dwarf flowering bulbs are especially comfortable. With dark red flowers, this thyme cultivar is outstanding. *Thymus praecox* var. *pseudolanuginosus*

(syn. *T. pseudolanuginosus*) develops an even more solid, gray and hairy cushion. Its pink flowers appear only individually, but its low mat soon covers entire rock formations or even the edge of a trough.

Veronica (Speedwell)

The several species of Speedwell form low, dense, and very hardy mats. I highly recommend *V. prostrata*, decorated in May and June with bright blue flowers. The form 'Alba' is also recommended.

Wulfenia

Wulfenia is a shrub with considerable appeal due to its shiny, green, leaf rosettes. In a semishaded trough or placed in the shaded part of a miniature rock garden, it will grow well and is decorated in May and June with blue-purple flower clusters.

Alpine Plants

Obtaining alpine, and especially rock plants is not nearly as simple as finding plants for the rock garden. Only a few sources exist. Imported plants often do not acclimate well. Often the only recourse is growing the plants from seed. Seeds are most easily obtained through the seed exchanges sponsored by various alpine and rock garden societies (see appendix).

Alpine plants demand careful planting and tending. Basic Mix B is the recommended planting medium. The advice in the chapter dealing with planting media and substrates should be followed to the letter in the case of rock plants.

Acantholimon

All species of *Acantholimon* are well suited for alpine rock gardens or troughs. They enjoy a sunny location, being planted in narrow crevices between rocks, and a very porous soil mixture, such as that of Basic Mix B. If these requirements have been met, *A. glumaceum*—with dense, stiff tufts bearing reddish pink flowers in late spring—and the floriferous *A. graminifolium*—producing reddish pink flowers arising from a softer foliage cushion—are bound to flourish. The silvery gray *A. olivieri* with reddish pink flowers grows more slowly and should be planted between rocks in a very well-drained trough, or else in the crevices of an alpine rock garden.

Achillea (Yarrow)

The mountain forms of Yarrow mostly have silvery gray cushions. Basic Mix A, amended with crushed rock, is recommended. I will highlight only a few from the multitudes of virtually identical forms.

Achillea ageratifolia is decorated in May with white flowers standing over silvery pillows; *A. kellereri* possesses a very beautiful fringed foliage cushion and is noted also for a long flowering period; *A. wilczeckii* is very attractive due to its pillows formed by large, tongue-shaped leaves. *Achillea umbellata* and *A. clavennae* are particularly treasured by collectors, together with many other species. Both are white-flowering with very attractive foliage cushions and require Basic Mix B amended with some gravel.

Aethionema (Stonecress)

The Stonecress species are attractive, spring-blooming plants for miniature gardens. Whether draped over the edge of a trough or squeezed between rocks, their requirements are uniform: Stonecress relishes a sunny, warm location and a planting medium well mixed with small rocks. They dislike standing water. Consequently, they are best planted in Basic Mix B amended with perlite, pumice, or other rock-derived materials.

The longest-lived species is *A. grandiflorum*. In spring the lilac-tinged pink flowers appear above attractive bluish gray foliage and produce a strong fragrance. *Aethionema warleyense* has a more needlelike foliage of a bluish gray hue. The flowers of 'Warley Rubrum' shine more brightly than those of the purplish pink 'Warley Rose'. *Aethionema oppositifolium* forms dense, diminutive mats when planted in porous Basic Mix B. Its lilac-pink flowers appear in May.

Alyssum

Apart from the well-known rock garden species of Alyssum, the spring-flowering *A. moellendorfianum*, making dense, silvery gray low carpets, looks splendid in a trough garden with its bright yellow flowers. Even on a flat spot between rocks, this species as well as *A. montanum* 'Berggold' can be used to advantage.

Anacyclus

Anacyclus depressus is a lovely plant for alpine rock gardens and troughs. Unfortunately, it has a short lifespan and will survive only with perfect drainage, particularly in the poor light of winter when the plant is very sensitive to moisture. A sunny location in water-permeable Basic Mix A or B is best for this plant. In spring, the reddish buds appear over finely divided, silvery foliage, eventually opening to white flowers.

Androsace (Rock Jasmine)

This genus contains a large number of noble alpine plants; their high-alpine representatives require particular attention and care. In permeable Basic Mix A soil, the Asiatic varieties fare very well. *Androsace sempervivoides* forms a dense, green mat of rosettes; in May the low-growing bright pink flowers appear. The loose-knitted carpet of rosettes typical of *A. primuloides* is hirsute and decorated with vibrant pink flowers in May. Another May-flowering species is *A. sarmentosa*, with carmine-pink flowers; its loose carpets cover entire rock formations. There are many cultivars of this species providing flowers from light to dark pink and whose rosettes vary in hairiness—for example 'Mollis', a very hairy form. The cushion of 'Sheriffii' distinguishes itself from the others by its spade-shaped and almost denuded rosettes.

A good transition plant for the beginner to the Rock Jasmine species found at higher elevations is *A. chamae-jasme*. The small cushions bear white flowers in May. This species does well in Basic Mix A, amended with considerable perlite or pumice. The same requirements hold for *A. villosa*. These species enjoy a location in rock crevices or on narrow ledges; *A. villosa* forms dense mats with many small, hairy rosettes and then develops white flowers in May. It also requires more care during planting and is not nearly as vigorous as *A. chamaejasme*. The small, dense rosettes of *A. villosa*, on the other hand, are more robust and have a strong, silvery stand of hair.

Every alpine plant lover's dream is to grow the high-alpine *Androsace* species. They are true jewels that survive by molding their very solid, dwarf tufts into the smallest rock crevices. It takes much skill to implant one of these tufts into the cracks or holes of a perforated limestone rock. It is best to use Basic Mix B, mixed 50:50 with coarse ground rock and topdressed with fine gravel around the stem. *Androsace pyrenaica* has a very

(**47**) White and yellow: *Minuartia laricifolia* and *Hieracium villosum*, with *Juniperus squamata* 'Blue Star' as the background. (**48**) *Picea pungens* 'Glauca globosa', accented by *Saxifraga trifurcata* and *Pinus sylvestris* 'Perkeo'. (**49**) *Roscoea cautleoides*, a Himalayan ginger orchid in a rock garden. (**50**) *Leontopodium alpinum* 'Alpengarten' is a superb Edelweiss cultivar. (**51**) Contrasts: light rock, Rock Pink, *Dianthus simulans* and *Sempervivum* 'Othello'. (**52**) Very pendulous and adhering tightly to the side of the trough is *Cotoneaster* 'Streibs Findling'.

beautiful and solid tuft covered even at low altitude with white flowers on very short stems; *A. imbricata* has a flatter foliage cushion. *Androsace helvetica*, a Swiss native, thrives only in narrow crevices covered completely with fine gravel and almost bereft of any humus. The roothairs of this plant should be planted in Basic Mix B, mixed with a bit of fine gravel.

Considerably easier to grow are the Asian species, *A. foliosa* and *A. strigillosa*. Planted in the well-draining material of Basic Mix A or B, they create large foliage rosettes with a very attractive appearance. The flowers are long-stemmed and pale white with a reddish pink reverse. From the Himalayas we also have *A. lanuginosa* 'Leichtlinii', which is highly recommended for its long flowering period. The plants form loose, open mats covered from summer until autumn with white flowers touched by a bit of lilac-pink. These varieties also grow well in porous Basic Mix A or B.

Andryala

Andryala agardhii enlivens an alpine garden with hirsute, whitish foliage and golden flowers that appear in early summer.

Anemone

The large white flowers of *A. narcissiflora* develop best on plants sited in shaded areas enriched with Basic Mix A. The related *A.* × *lesseri* has carmine-red flowers and prefers the same growing conditions.

Anemone alpina and *A. pulsatilla* see *Pulsatilla*

Anthemis

For alpine miniature gardens, *A. biebersteiniana* is the best choice. In late spring, golden yellow flowers appear on 4–5 in. (10–12 cm) tall stems. The finely divided, silver foliage is attractive even without these flowers. *Anthemis barrelieri* requires protection from winter moisture. The silvery gray cushions thrive in Basic Mix B, so long as it has been amended with perlite or pumice.

Aquilegia (Columbine)

The lower-growing *Aquilegia* species provide a lovely appearance in a lightly-shaded spot. They appreciate being planted among loosely creeping cushion plants, for example between *Minuartia* and the loose mats of *Veronica*. A solid groundcover around the plants is also of advantage. All low varieties are suitable, and they fare well in Basic Mix A. *Aquilegia flabellata* (syn. *A. akitensis*) has two forms, 'Nana' and 'Mini Star', characterized by a very dwarf habit and rather large, blue flowers. Very large, but lighter blue flowers are the trademark of *A. glandulosa*. Small, violet flowers and a delicate, finely divided foliage identify *A. einseleana*. The graceful *A. canadensis* is a yellow and red bicolor. Finally, the bright multicolored *A. caerulea* 'Biedermeier' is characterized by a robust yet low-growing habit.

Arabis (Rockcress)

As essential as Rockcress species are in the design of a cheerful rock garden, they are also very useful in alpine settings when dense, green mats between rocks and rock formations are called for. In partly shaded areas *A. scopoliana* weaves dark green carpets which are covered with white flowers in May. Dwarf, hoary cushions are created by *A. androsacea* as it squeezes between rocks, while *A. pumila* and *A. vochinensis* spread their tiny green leaves in lightly shaded areas. All these species thrive in troughs in partial shade or between alpine rock formations and prefer Basic Mix A.

Arenaria (Sandwort)

Dense, stiff, dwarf clumps with almost vertically arranged flowers are formed by *A. tetraquetra*. This Sandwort feels most comfortable in tight spaces, rock crevices, and a sunny location. It blooms in the spring. Less dense, but with very large, pure white flowers is *A. montana* 'Grandiflora' which forms green cushions between rocks. In May and June, *A. ledebouriana* is decorated with elegant, white flowers standing over loosely knit, bluish green foliage cushions. *Arenaria sajanensis*, a low, dense dwarf cushion is—together with the pale pink blooming, loose-patterned *A. purpurascens*—a suitable groundcover in shaded sites.

Armeria (Thrift)

Apart from the widely used cultivars of *A. maritima*, for alpine gardens *A. juniperifolia* (syn. *A. caespitosa*) comes to mind. This *Armeria* develops dense, short-leaved green cushions; in spring, short-stemmed globular pink flowers appear. Other color selections—dark pink, pink, and white—are also available and are all short stemmed. Thrift does best in narrow crevices and in Basic Mix A. More vigorous is *A. suendermannii*, with longer-stemmed, dark pink blossoms.

Artemisia

Finely divided fronds of silvery white foliage are a noteworthy characteristic of *A. schmidtiana* 'Nana', which likes a sunny location among some rocks, although it is somewhat more difficult to grow. Make sure that all superfluous moisture can run off during the autumn and winter months. *Artemisia assoana* forms somewhat larger silver cushions; *A. umbelliformis* (syn. *A. laxa*), on the other hand, displays only small, shiny dwarf cushions, as does *A. nitida*.

Asperula

Several species are suitable for planting in troughs or rock gardens. Very undemanding is *A. lilaciflora* 'Caespitosa', a lovely and very short cushion plant, which is covered in spring with intensively reddish pink flowers when planted in a sunny location. Whether this plant falls over the edge of a trough, or emerges from between narrow crevices, or even when its cushion oozes out of the holes of perforated limestone while displaying its lovely flower truss, it is a treasure in the alpine garden. *Asperula cynanchica* decorates its loose mats early in summer with fragrant, light pink flowers.

Aster

Most *Aster* species are robust shrubs for rock gardens or the flower bed. *Aster natalense* is well suited for alpine plantings, together with *A. alpinus*, the Alpine Aster. The pure blue flowers rise in early summer 4–6 in. (10–15 cm) above the low, dark green foliage clump.

Astragalus

Very sensitive to moisture, *Astragalus* species require Basic Mix B, well mixed with small rock chips, and a place in full sun. *Astragalus angustifolius* forms stiff cushions; the cream-colored flowers appear in late spring. *Astragalus monspessulanus* has purplish red blooms, its foliage is less dense, and the greenery drapes over alpine rock formations in a picturesque fashion.

Azorella

Dense, solid, and shiny green cushions characterize *A. trifurcata*. The greenish white, dense and upright flowers appear in early summer. This alpine plant from the Andes creates beautiful solid mats in sunny locations.

Calceolaria

Calceolaria species suitable for alpine treatment prefer locations that are not too dry and yet covered with coarse gravel to permit the plant to survive the winter in relative dryness. *Calceolaria polyrrhiza* creates somewhat larger foliage cushions and is decorated in summer with yellow flower trusses. Small, flat, shiny foliage rosettes are a characteristic of *C. biflora,* which also has golden yellow flowers.

Callianthemum

Collectors of alpine flowers and plants should not overlook this genus. The white blossoms of *C. anemonoides* appear early in spring over immature leaves; the foliage eventually grows into feathery tufts. Somewhat later flowering is the similar *C. coriandrifolium.*

Campanula (Bellflower)

Bellflowers—particularly the alpine varieties—are essential plants in any alpine garden. Unfortunately, the low-growing varieties are particularly attractive to slugs, so that continued preventative treatment with slug bait is advised. The Dwarf Bellflower, *C. cochleariifolia* (syn. *C. pusilla*), sports delicate blue bells. New tufts are created between rocks in the narrowest of crevices by subsurface runners. This new growth is covered with flowers during the spring blooming period. Be careful when using *Campanula* in troughs: spreading runners will, in time, interfere with other plants and can

(*53*) *Armeria juniperifolia* and an early-flowering saxifrage of Section Kabschia. (*54*) Flat trough, planted with *Sempervivum* exclusively: from front to back—*S. blandum* and *S. arachnoideum* ssp. *tomentosum*, plus *S.* 'Rubin'. (*55*) *Sempervivum* 'Othello' next to *S. arachnoideum* ssp. *tomentosum*. (*56*) "Cat's Head" on a small grinding wheel has character even without plants. (*57*) Planter with winter-hardy cactus *Opuntia polyacantha*, in front *Sempervivum* 'Maby'. (*58*) *Sempervivum* 'Purpurriese' with *Opuntia humifusa*. *Opuntia* cactus and *Sempervivum* always look good together.

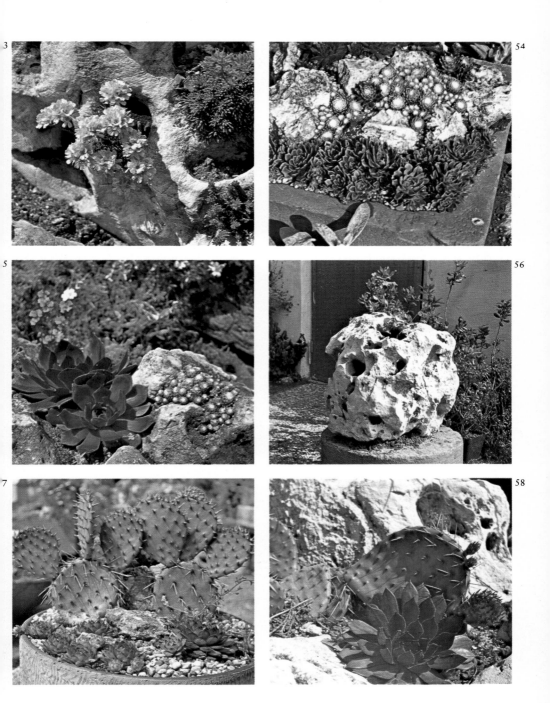

take over. One of the prettiest and most graceful of the bellflowers for troughs is *C. portenschlagiana* 'Birch Hybrid'. With its light lavender-blue bells, which appear during May and June, this cultivar is a focal point in any garden. Star-shaped lavender bells are the mark of *C. garganica*, which is native to Dalmatia. Its heavy flowering and undemanding habit make this species an essential.

Somewhat more demanding are the alpine species. *Campanula cashmiriana* blooms the entire summer—in the winter season, though, moisture is certain poison. The dwarf alpine species *C. excisa*, *C. morettiana* and *C. zoysii* surprise with their large flowers which appear in summer over the sparse, dwarf shoots. All prefer partial shade and a location in very coarse soil mixed with crushed gravel next to larger rocks.

Chiastophyllum

Set out between rocks in a shady location, *C. oppositifolium* is well suited for an alpine planting. The yellow, pendulous panicles rise in summer over round, fleshy leaves.

Chrysanthemum

Aside from the somewhat difficult *C. alpinum*, the white-flowering Alpine Marguerite, *C. weyrichii*, is noteworthy for its relatively easy adaptation to trough or rock gardens. In early summer, the short-stemmed, large, reddish pink blooms appear over shiny green, dense foliage cushions.

Codonopsis

In a trough or a slab garden, or perhaps when placed among rock formations, the plants of this genus really stand out. Preferably the plant should be at a level to permit one to see inside the flower bell to admire the lovely marbling of the interior. *Codonopsis clematidea* flowers—as do all species of this genus—during summer; its porcelain blue bells display a brownish yellow pattern in their interior. *Codonopsis meleagris* has cream-colored flowers with reddish brown interiors, while *C. ovata* has azure-blue and dark-veined blooms.

Cyclamen

Shaded sites in alpine rock gardens are ideal for hardy cyclamens. The light and humusy Basic Mix A is their preferred growing medium. Grown between rocks, on broad, shaded sites next to dwarf shrubs, the autumn-flowering species will fare well. *Cyclamen purpurascens* (syn. *C. europaeum*) has carmine-red blossoms that appear in August and September; its foliage sports characteristically kidney-shaped leaves with pale silver markings. Lanceolate leaves with strong, silvery gray markings identify the foliage of the very hardy pink-flowering *C. hederifolium* (syn. *C. linearifolium*, *C. neapolitanum*). Its flowering period is from September to October. *Cyclamen coum*, on the other hand, is a spring-flowering species available in carmine-pink, pink, and also a white-flowering form, 'Album'. This form should not be planted too deeply, but rather the tuber barely covered. While autumn-flowering species grow well in shaded troughs, *C. coum* requires some mulching with leaves or peat for winter protection.

Cymbalaria

I recommend *C. muralis* (syn. *Linaria cymbalaria*) 'Globosa Rosea' for an alpine garden. The dense, ball-shaped and compact foliage cushions display lilac-pink blossoms all summer long; at the same time, it is not as invasive as the species. This cultivar thrives in Basic Mix A, but cannot stand much moisture during the winter months.

Dianthus (Pink)

Among the most important species for alpine rock gardens are those belonging in the *Dianthus* genus. The Rock Pink types usually form dense, stiff tufts that are attractive all year long, even after flowering. Among the rock-growing *Dianthus* there are any number of dwarf species with relatively large flowers on short stems. These thrive in full sun and light, permeable soil (Basic Mix A).

Dianthus gratianopolitanus (syn. *D. caesius*) has very dense, low-flowering forms, such as 'Blaureif' or 'Compactus'; both have reddish pink flowers and are very well suited for troughs. *Dianthus arenarius* is a pretty, white, early summer-flowering species with dense, gray-green foliage. Gorgeous, large, reddish pink blossoms on very short stems are the major feature of 'La Bourbrille'; it is a hybrid of undetermined origin whose mounded blue-gray foliage sits prettily among the rocks. *Dianthus simulans* also forms a low and dense dwarf cushion. Its flowers are somewhat smaller, but they are also a striking dark pink. What a beautiful sight, when such a clump grows over the edge of a trough or oozes out of the holes of a perforated rock! Another species worthy of consideration is *D. pavonicus* (syn. *D. neglectus*) with its wine-red blooms, or the taller *D. sylvestris*, a floriferous reddish pink. In late July and August, *D. petraeus* ssp. *noeanus* (syn. *D. noeanus*) blooms with white, somewhat fimbriated flowers. It develops very

lovely, solid, green mounds and is very durable. Tiny dwarf species are the reddish pink *D. microlepis* and the even more diminutive *D. musalae*. Both enjoy a location next to rocks. Of the dwarf species, *D. alpinus* has the largest flower, but only experienced growers of alpines can provide the ideal conditions for this short-lived plant. Its worst enemy is too much soil moisture; at the same time, too dry a soil does not suit it either. Basic Mix B amended with an equal measure of gravel, together with a partly-shaded location, are the best guarantee for satisfactory growth.

Dodecatheon (Shooting Star)

Very beautiful, unusual flower clusters on solid stems but a virtual lack of a foliage cushion characterize the Shooting Star, a native of North America. *Dodecatheon meadia* is the best-known species with its lilac-pink blossoms which look much like cyclamen at a distance. The hybrid 'Red Wings', with bright carmine-red flowers, is as useful as other species and cultivars. They prefer Basic Mix A, even in troughs. After flowering, the plant's basal rosettes virtually dry up and disappear.

Douglasia see Vitaliana

Draba

This genus does not require much in the way of care or special soil. The plant grows in very small crevices or narrow holes in limestone and forms dense dwarf rosettes even in the poorest of soils. *Draba lasiocarpa* and *D. aizoides* decorate their dense, small cushions in early spring with golden yellow flowers. *Draba bruniifolia* var. *diversifolia* is particularly heavy-blooming and grows steadily. One of the prettiest *Draba* species is, of course, *D. olympica* (Sibth.) non hort. with very large flowers and short stems. Do not confuse it with the more generally-available longer-stemmed species *D. bruniifolia* (syn. *D. olympica* hort.). *Draba* × *suendermannii* has white flowers and also forms dense dwarf cushions.

There are many other species; all are suitable for an alpine display because of dense dwarf cushion habit and their preference for the friable Basic Mix A.

A couple of species are recommended strictly for experienced growers because of their susceptibility to winter moisture. *Draba mollissima* and *D. polytricha* fare well in an alpine greenhouse or under appropriate cover. The golden yellow blossoms of *D. mollissima* develop over silvery gray dwarf mounds in early spring; *D. polytricha* has green foliage. Both prefer a very gravelly and water-permeable soil (best to use Basic Mix B).

Dryas

This is a typical alpine plant. It is actually a dwarf shrub, but is generally listed under perennials. This very long-lived plant is desirable because of its dense, mat-forming habit, and because the foliage spills over the side of a trough or covers entire rock formations. *Dryas octopetala*, the alpine species, is slow growing with white flowers. Another white-flowering species with richer flowers and more vigorous growth is *D. suendermannii*. *Dryas drummondi* has yellow buds which open to creamy white flowers. Even after flowering, the seed capsules are attractive with their silvery white plumes.

Edraianthus

These are ideal plants for tight cracks between rocks and for perforated limestone. All species prefer sunny locations and Basic Mix A, mixed with some sand. One of the prettiest is *E. dinaricus*. It forms

(59) Trough made of washed aggregate and planted with Arolla Pine, *P. cembra*, and Spreading Juniper, *J. chinensis* 'Old Gold', accompanied by begonias and lantana. (60) An alpine trough looks attractive even when nothing is in flower. Here is an example with *Sempervivum* 'Othello' and Rock Pink, *Dianthus simulans*. (61) Another example, with *Picea pungens* 'Glauca Globosa' and Dwarf Pine, *Pinus sylvestris* 'Perkeo', which form the structure of the landscape; in front are *Cotoneaster* 'Streib's Findling' and *Acantholimon glumaceum*.

dense, grayish green cushions and is decorated in early summer with *Campanula*-like blue, short-stemmed flowers in great number. Just as hardy are *E. graminifolius* and *E. tenuifolius;* both have somewhat longer stems with violet flowers and prefer locations in the vicinity of rocks.

Experienced growers may also wish to try *E. pumilio.* It is much like *E. dinaricus* in all respects. The large, lilac flowers sit on barely noticeable short stems. Loose dwarf cultivars and large single, dark violet flowers mark *E. serpyllifolius.* Its form 'Albo-Violacea' is particularly enticing; displaying almost white, delicately blue-hued flowers. *Edraianthus serpyllifolius* should be located in partial shade. For those species and cultivars of interest to collectors, a very porous mix of Basic Mix B is recommended.

Erigeron (Fleabane)

Apart from the many garden varieties, there are several species suited for alpine miniature gardens. *Erigeron leiomerus* forms green, dense, low clumps but only displays a few lilac-blue flowers; *E. aurantiacus,* on the other hand, has relatively large golden flowers. I can also recommend *E. radicatus* for rock gardens or alpine troughs with very porous soil of Basic Mix B. This species displays lovely small, blue flowers over very small leaves.

Erinus

Erinus alpinus 'Dr. Hähnle' provides bright and beautiful focal points in spring. The low, small, and dense leaf cushions are studded with carmine-red blossoms. The white *E. alpinus* 'Albus' is just as desirable.

Eriogonum

All *Eriogonum* species can stand full sun and droughty conditions. The following also flower during the summer and do well in Basic Mix A: *E. racemosum* forms a dense, gray-green clump; the sparse flower clusters are pinkish white. Green foliage and yellow flower clusters identify *E. umbellatum. Eriogonum jamesii* blooms heavier (golden yellow) but does not have as sturdy a foliage structure.

Erodium

The summer-flowering *Erodium* species make very handsome plants in troughs and alpine rock gardens. The geranium-like blossoms appear throughout the season over finely divided, mostly gray foliage. The flowers are a delicate pinkish white with dark rosy veining in the case of *E. petraeum* ssp. *crispum* (syn. *E. cheilanthifolium*). On the other hand, *E. chrysanthum* blooms pale yellow, while *E. sibthorpianum* has pink flowers. Recommended only for very dry locations with little winter moisture and very porous soil of Basic Mix A or B, *E. reichardii* (syn. *E. chamaedryoides*) really does best in an alpine greenhouse or covered alpine garden. Its cultivar 'Roseum' makes a low-growing, dense pillow with reddish pink blossoms, having virtually no stem; another, 'Plenum', is double.

Euphorbia (Spurge)

The only *Euphorbia* species suitable for alpine plantings is *E. capitulata.* It grows willingly and forms dense, green-blue clumps among the rocks. Its flowers are a greenish yellow and appear in early summer.

Euryops

Euryops evansii, a low-growing shrub, is attractive even after flowering due to its silvery gray foliage. In early summer it is decorated with large, yellow blossoms. *Euryops* requires sun and Basic Mix A or B, amended with some crushed gravel.

Galium (Woodruff)

Galium baldense forms thick, mossy green clumps in very porous Basic Mix B; in summer these plants are covered with delicate, small, white blossoms. *Galium olympicum,* which has even more delicate foliage, prefers the interstices between rocks; *G. incanum* decorates crevices and small ledges with its dense, grayish green, dwarf foliage.

Gentiana (Gentian)

Apart from Edelweiss, gentian is one of the best-known alpine flowers and should not be left off any plant list for troughs, slab gardens, or rock gardens. The selection of appropriate gentians, though, is difficult for the layman since there are so many species. The low-growing species are the first choice for a hardy garden, especially *G. acaulis*—the stemless gentian of the Alps. Of this large-flowering, bright blue species there are many cultivars that are appealing to the plant collector. One of the easiest and most heavily blooming is 'Dinarica'; other good cultivars are 'Gedanensis', ultramarine blue, and 'Holzmannii', azure-blue. 'Undulatifolia' has interesting wavy foliage.

All gentians thrive in Basic Mix A. The dark blue flowers of *G. kurroo* appear on prostrate, long stems; *G. decumbens* has blooms of a lighter hue. The late-summer-flowering species *G. septemfida* has forms that are just as hardy as the parent; con-sider, therefore, 'Doeringiana', a darker selection, and the more upright-growing 'Erecta'.

The Chinese treasures called Autumn Gentians, of Section Frigidae, bloom beautifully and thrive in a mixture of equal parts Basic Mixes A and D. However, unlike other gentians, these prefer some shade—just not too much. The best-growing hybrid is *G. × macaulayi,* a cross between *G. farreri* and *G. sino-ornata.* The large flowers of *G. farreri* shine in a bright azure-blue, veined in a darker shade on the tube's exterior. Coarser foliage is found on *G. sino-ornata.* Its equally large flowers are a deep azure color with even darker veining.

A great number of cultivars have been made, many of which are indistinguishable from one another. Their flower colors range from pure, translucent blue to a dark cobalt-blue. Cultural require-

Gorgeous blue flowers are typical of the Stemless Gentian, *G. acaulis.*

105

ments are the same for all these forms so that they can be selected from nursery catalogs with little trepidation.

The most beautiful and brightest blue is found on the spring-flowering gentian G. *verna*. This species has to be tended with greater care and is not easy to cultivate over the long term. Nevertheless, it will do well in troughs or between the stones of a rock garden, so long as it gets what it needs: careful tending; humus-enriched, permeable soil of Basic Mix B or a sandy-gravelly Basic Mix A; a plant site that never dries out during summer; and finally, frequent light misting. Another plant recommended strictly for the experienced is G. *bavarica*, whose basal rosettes are more rounded than those of G. *verna*. Its striking deep blue flower tubes will move any alpine plant lover. This species also dislikes the dry, warm climate of lowland areas. Consequently, it must receive sufficient and regular moisture in summer, yet over-saturation must be avoided.

Geranium

Geranium species are another essential group for troughs and other miniature gardens. *Geranium dalmaticum* creates low, dense mats of attractive, roundish leaves spreading lustily between the rocks. In summer, silky reddish pink blooms decorate the plant. Its white sport 'Album' is also lovely. Just as essential and long-blooming is G. *subcaulescens* 'Splendens'. While it does not form large mats, the carmine-red blooms can be enjoyed all summer long. This cultivar is best suited for planting in deep holes of perforated limestone. Another particularly blooming cultivar is G. *cinereum* 'Ballerina'. Its flowers are light purplish pink and open atop decorative foliage. All forms prefer Basic Mix A.

Geum

Only the low G. *montanum* should be considered for miniature gardens. Its yellow flowers appear in late spring to early summer.

(*62*) Evergreen groundcover with Blue Juniper, *Juniperus horizontalis* 'Glauca', and Yew, *Taxus media* 'Hicksii', in the background, combined with colorful summer flowers. (*63*) Bellflowers grow well in alpine gardens. *Campanula portenschlagiana* 'Birch Hybrid' has particularly pretty bells and a long flowering period. (*64*) *Sempervivum* species are uniformly attractive largely due to their nicely formed rosettes and their star-shaped flowers on thick, fleshy stems. This *S. arachnoideum* ssp. *tomentosum* proves the point.

Globularia

Dark green, dense mats are characteristic of *G. cordifolia*. During the flowering period in late spring, blue flower heads dot the foliage clumps. This hardy and long-lived plant is very useful along the edges of troughs. Considerably more vigorous is *G. lindavica*, displaying its blue, globe flowers. *Globularia repens* (syn. *G. nana*)—the dwarf amongst the globularias—is particularly suitable for perforated limestone. Growing in Basic Mix B, this plant forms small, dense, dwarf mats covering crevices and holes with stemless, light blue blossoms.

Gymnandra see Lagotis

Gypsophila

Aside from the taller *Gypsophila*, numerous lower-growing species exist which are suitable for alpine gardens. An example is *G. cerastioides*, whose low, open mats are covered in spring with large white flowers, veined in lilac. Plant *G. aretioides* in narrow crevices, or better yet on perforated limestone. This very slow-growing species hugs the surrounding rock and attains its real beauty only after growing in one location for several years. More delicate and of weaker growth habit is the form 'Caucasica'. *Gypsophila tenuifolia* prefers crevices or perforated limestone as well; once established, it spreads out in dense, green mats.

Haberlea

In late spring, *H. rhodopensis* displays bell-shaped flowers of a delicate lilac color over interesting looking foliage rosettes. Always select a site in partial shade for these plants. They thrive in Basic Mix D or a mixture of D and B. The form 'Viminalis' bears white flowers with yellow-spotted throats.

Helianthemum

The dwarf forms of *Helianthemum* make beautiful, dense mats. They thrive in sunny locations. *Helianthemum oelandicum* ssp. *alpestre* (syn. *H. alpestre*) 'Serpyllifolium' bears bright yellow flowers in early summer atop a foliage carpet composed of small, dark green leaves. A similar dwarf cover is characteristic of *H. oelandicum*, whose yellow flowers appear in late spring. Grayish green, low, dwarf foliage mats typify *H. canum*; like the similar *H. scardicum*, this species also has bright yellow flowers. Somewhat higher in growth is the bushy *H. lunulatum*, a Rock Rose with grayish blue foliage and golden flowers tinged with orange. All the named cultivars are perfect for enlivening the edge of troughs or rock formations with pendulous, hardy mats.

Helichrysum

A jewel for any alpine garden is *H. milfordiae*. This species exhibits its beautiful, silvery gray, thick pillows to greatest advantage when planted on perforated limestone or between the cracks of a rock formation. The large flowers are pale pink at first, then turn white; they open early in summer on short stems and over thick foliage rosettes. This plant is very susceptible to wetness during winter so requires fast drainage and Basic Mix B.

Helichrysum sibthorpii (syn. *H. virgineum*) has very attractive, large, white and woolly leaf rosettes. Another, *H. frigidum*, is more diminutive in all respects and its flowers a silvery white with yellowish centers. These species all grow especially well in an alpine greenhouse or covered alpine garden.

Hieracium (Hawkweed)

As beautiful as the red or orange-yellow flowers of *H. rubrum* and *H. aurantiacum* may be, the plants tend to become invasive and spread in all directions. Only *H. bombycinum* and *H. villosum* have a tidy habit. Their very attractive foliage is covered with a white fuzz, and both bear yellow flowers early in summer.

Hippocrepis (Horseshoe Vetch)

The gardener seeking a plant that is right for hanging over the edge of a trough, and one that is also hardy and long-lived, should try *H. comosa*. During the summer, the draping mats are decorated with golden yellow flowers with reddish overtones.

Horminum

Horminum pyrenaicum is formed by large leaf rosettes; in late spring, violet-colored flower clusters rise from among the wrinkled foliage. This plant is not at all demanding and grows nearly everywhere, regardless of lighting.

Hutchinsia

White flower clusters stand over delicate green mats during early summer wherever *H. alpina* thrives. The related *H. alpina* ssp. *auerswaldii* (syn. *H. auerswaldii*) is more floriferous. Both thrive in somewhat moist locations in an alpine setting.

Iberis (Candytuft)

The creeping *I. saxatilis* is essential for the planting of a trough. Early in spring the dense mounds are covered with numerous, white flowers. Daintier and even smaller is *I. pygmaea*; this one fits well into the crevices of a trough or alpine slab garden. *Iberis candolleana*, another very

flat, dwarf form, has short, needlelike foliage. All these species are spring flowering and prosper in Basic Mix A or B.

Incarvillea (Hardy Gloxinia)

Though growing only to a height of 8–12 in. (20–30 cm), *I. mairei* takes a very prominent place in a trough or slab garden, thanks to its interesting flowers. These large, carmine-pink blossoms appear in late spring. In late summer the plant foliage completely disappears. However, the fleshy rootstock is so robust that new growth and blooms appear the following spring. *Incarvillea* prefers Basic Mix A. Several color forms are available; for example, there is the deep pink-blooming 'Frank Rudlow', the light pink 'Nyoto Sama', and the large-flowering 'Bees Pink'.

Iris

Virtually all the irises deserve a place in the flower garden; however, only the low-growing species are suited for rock garden culture, and several even do well in alpine collections. The large yellow blossoms of the low-growing *I. danfordiae* appear as early as March. Soon after, the deep lavender flowers of *I. reticulata* open. This species has many good cultivars which can be grown in miniature gardens. I can heartily recommend *I. cristata*; its rhizomatous roots form compact carpets, and the foliage is decorated with low-blooming lilac flowers. This species, as well as the more delicate *I. lacustris* which blooms in a lighter shade of blue, thrives in sandy Basic Mix A. Both species flower in late spring. *Iris japonica* is an attractive, though more sensitive, species with light azure-blue flowers. It grows particularly well in covered alpine gardens or in a greenhouse devoted to alpines. The recommended planting medium for this iris is Basic Mix A.

Jovibarba

Jovibarba heuffelii is very beautiful and is still often found in nursery catalogs under its old name *Sempervivum heuffelii*. The green rosettes have brownish red tips. The plant produces no offsets for propagation, and the individual rosettes are located so close to each other that division is very difficult.

Lagotis

In spring, *L. stolonifera* (syn. *Gymnandra stolonifera*) sports beautiful blue flowers. The shiny green foliage clumps develop long runners, at the ends of which new plants appear.

Leontopodium

If the gardener is intent on growing truly beautiful and noble, hirsute Edelweiss flowers in the lowlands, he can do so most easily in a trough or alpine garden. In the first instance, proper plant selection is essential. What is usually offered as *L. alpinum* is derived from seedlings started from cultivated garden plants, so their habit and flowering are quite variable. The true Edelweiss *L. alpinum* remains dwarf, even when growing in the lowlands, and hairy, well-formed flower stars poke out from hirsute, whitish foliage clumps. Such plants are derived from seeds collected in the wild and often offered as *L. alpinum vera*. The plants require particularly porous soil. Basic Mix A, or even better, Basic Mix B is mixed nearly 50:50 with pumice, perlite, or coarse crushed gravel.

(65) Clinging tightly to the rock surface of perforated limestone is a white-flowering form of *Draba* × *suendermannii*. All *Draba* species are very well suited for planting in this way. (66) Light-colored limestone shows off *Sempervivum* 'Purpurriese' to exceptional advantage. The Bellflower, *Campanula cochleariifolia*, is comfortable in the tightest spaces; however, it may take over quickly. (67) Semicircular trough with Saxifrage, *Sempervivum*, and a Marsh Lily. Rocks and an old root provide transitions between the different genera but at the same time separate them.

This species is not usually long-lived, but the elegant, flawless blossoms more than compensate. If a less difficult plant is wanted, I recommend *L. souliei*, a Himalayan species that is perfect for gardens. The plants appear to be greener, and the flower stars that appear in summer are never too large and have a beautiful, silver fuzz. The form 'Mignon' has shorter flower stems, and the plant is a bit stouter. Both grow very willingly and thrive in Basic Mix A in any trough, planter, or window box.

In addition to these species that should be considered first, there are a number of other forms. Several selections of *L. alpinum* are available; all are very useful, so long as they are vegetatively propagated and not from seeds. A particularly beautiful and good cultivar is the recent introduction 'Alpengarten'. This plant, which grows only 2–3 in. (5–7 cm) high, is noted for its very regular growth,

In June, the starry flowers of *Leontopodium alpinum*, the Alpine Edelweiss, appear.

frequency of flowering, and the well-formed, single blossoms which are especially hairy. It develops well-shaped, compact clumps covered with perfectly formed white flowers. The Asiatic species, such as *L. himalayanum* with its very large flower stars; *L. palibinianum*, a late bloomer; and *L. stracheyi* also with very large flowers, thrive in porous soil with a minimum of nutrients.

Lewisia

The pride of every lover of alpine plants, and the yardstick of his or her knowledge, are the *Lewisia*. Not at all simple to care for, these plants excite with their gorgeous flower clusters, which appear late in spring. From autumn until early spring, *Lewisia* requires protection from too much moisture. They are frequently kept in pots, in order that they can be relocated under cover during the winter months. They develop particularly well in covered rock gardens or the alpine greenhouse. But *Lewisia* also thrives in troughs and slab gardens, in narrow cracks with excellent drainage. Lewisias truly enjoy a place in perforated limestone or tufa; the key to successful growing is superb drainage resulting from a very porous planting medium. Keep the area in the immediate vicinity of the stem free of humus, providing instead a top dressing of several inches of fine stone chips or other fine rock material. If water can run off through this rock layer very quickly and disappear in the lower layers of the soil, then lewisias develop with abandon.

The species with evergreen leaf rosettes should be tried first, beginning with lewisias in troughs. Of these, the easiest to grow is *L. cotyledon*. Its white-pink striped, branched flower clusters appear in late spring over rosettes formed from broad, spade-shaped leaves. This species has many good forms; most have single-colored flowers, usually salmon-pink to pink, but also dark reddish pink. The reddish pink *L. heckneri* has a rosette of narrow, slightly wavy and serrated leaves. *Lewisia cotyledon* var. *howellii* has very wavy foliage and gorgeous, brilliant, apricot-colored flower clusters. All of these species flower from late spring into early summer.

For the *cognoscenti* and alpine collectors, let me mention *L. nevadense* and *L. rediviva*, Bitterroot. Both species die back after flowering. They too require a very porous medium and cannot stand much moisture. Their white flowers appear in early summer on short stems over the narrow, compact leaf rosettes. A particular prize is *L. tweedyi*, whose expansive leaf rosettes are decorated in late spring with large, delicate salmon-pink flowers. As with all other lewisias, these tend to develop their full beauty primarily in covered locations or in an alpine greenhouse.

Linaria (Toadflax)

Linaria alpina, the Alpine Toadflax, is a typical inhabitant of scree slopes or rock fields. It prefers coarse rock, amended with Basic Mix A. It shows off its purple-blue flowers throughout the summer. Be sure to also consider the beautiful form 'Rosea', whose violet-pink flowers are spotted with orange-yellow accents.

Linaria cymbalaria see Cymbalaria

Linum (Flax)

A low-growing species, *L. perenne* ssp. *alpinum* (syn. *L. alpinum*) is especially well suited for alpine miniature gardens. The blue blossoms of Flax appear throughout summer, and the plant willingly grows in Basic Mix A. Somewhat greater attention and care is required by *L. capitatum*, a low, bushy plant with beautiful, bluish green foliage and golden yellow summer flowers. Also yellow-flowering is *L. viscosum*. Both species need somewhat protected locations in porous Basic Mix A or B.

Lotus

Lotus corniculatus 'Plenus' is a very robust and durable cushion plant that bears its golden yellow double flowers all summer long over compact, green foliage cushions.

Marrubium

Those who treasure unusual foliage should plant *M. supinum* in a trough or an alpine rock garden. The silvery gray clumps composed of roundish, soft, and woolly leaves look attractive the year round. The small, lilac-pink flowers appear during the summer.

Meconopsis

The various *Meconopsis* species look their best in an alpine rock garden setting. These are lovely perennials whose flower stems may grow to 1 yd. (1 m) long, but which cannot be omitted from any alpine miniature garden collection because they produce not only beautiful flowers but low, yet attractive leaf rosettes as well. All species prefer a location in partial shade. During the period of active growth, these plants can also stand a bit more moisture; during winter, though, they demand nearly dry soil. A quick-draining amended form of Basic Mix A is perfect.

The leaf rosettes of *M. betonicifolia* are covered with brownish hair; in early summer the pale blue flowers appear. *Meconopsis horridula* has steel-blue flowers, *M. napaulensis* usually purple-red, and *M. paniculata*, yellow.

Mentha (Mint)

Mentha requienii, a dwarf mint from Corsica, tends to form very low, dense carpets in partial shade or in shaded trough gardens; the foliage gives off a fragrant peppermint odor when the leaves are brushed. Small violet flowers appear in summer. This plant enjoys a moist location and will surround dwarf shrubs or rhododendrons with a dense, green carpet.

Micromeria

The summer-flowering micromerias belong in the holes of perforated limestone in trough gardens, or between the rocks of a rock garden. One is grateful for the late blooming period—they bear their interesting little flowers well into autumn. *Micromeria croatica* is a small, fragrant shrub with light purple-red flowers, while *M. microphylla's* flowers are pink.

Minuartia

Apart from the very vigorous *M. laricifolia*, *M. graminifolia* should always be considered for planting in rock crevices, although it hardly ever flowers. However, its dense, flat, and green dwarf cushions hug rocks and boulders tightly and slowly spread out durable green mats. A looser matting habit and white flowers mark *M. subnivalis*.

Moltkia

Moltkia really could be considered a flowering, dwarf shrub. Characterized by a bushy, compact growth and bright dark blue flowers, *M.* × *intermedia* is a jewel in rocks and rock crevices during the summer. *M. petraea* has violet-blue flowers. Both species prefer a sunny, warm location in quick-draining Basic Mix A.

Nierembergia

The large-flowered, white species *N. repens* (syn. *N. rivularis*) prefers light shade and some moisture. Its cushions are compact and grassy, and the short-stemmed flowers appear from summer into autumn.

Ononis

The alpine version of *O. cristata* (syn. *O. cenisia*) hugs rocks and forms small, matlike cushions. Pink flowers with a white infusion appear in late summer.

Onosma

Gorgeous, pendulous mats composed of coarse-haired narrow leaves are the most visible characteristic of *Onosma*; its prettiest species is *O. albo-rosea*. As the name indicates, the bell-shaped, tubular flowers are delicately white and in the coarse of bloom begin to turn pink from the fringe downward. *Onosma stellulata* is looser growing and has yellow flowers. A garden site can never be too warm for *Onosma*; they also require excellent drainage.

Opuntia

A trough containing succulents should incorporate not only *Sempervivum* but also hardy cactus species, such as the opuntias. The most important precondition here is rapid drainage and protection from excess moisture during winter. Cover opuntias with conifer bows without fail should killer frosts or the much-feared late frosts of spring be expected. Very hardy species include: *O. humifusa*, flowers light yellow and profuse; *O. phaecantha* var. *camanchica*, light orange-yellow flowers; and *O. rhodantha*, light carmine-red flowers.

Origanum

Origanum amanum, a pretty, low, summer-flowering plant with reddish pink flowers, develops especially well in alpine greenhouses in sunny sites and where the plants can be protected from winter precipitation. *Origanum laevigatum* can be highly recommended for slab gardens or for planting between rock formations. This species flowers in late summer and autumn; the flowers are a violet-purple. While plants do not remain dwarf and low, but begin to grow rangy, the late flowering period makes origanums very desirable.

Orostachys

Similar to *Sempervivum* in appearance, *O. spinosus* is a round rosette plant that fits readily between rocks and is well-suited for planting in the hollows of tufa or per-forated limestone.

Paederota

Paederota bonarota (syn. *Veronica bonarota*) thrives in perforated rock or in rock formations. The lilac flower clusters appear in summer. *Paederota* prefers some shade.

Papaver (Poppy)

Only when planted in a well-drained trough or on the scree of a rock garden does *P. alpinum* develop its full beauty. Its large flowers—white, yellow, orange, and pink—wave over low-growing, finely divided, bluish green foliage throughout the summer. Once again, the most important cultural condition is that these species require protection from winter moisture; otherwise, they rot. The alpine plant aficionado values the special forms of *P. alpinum*, such as 'Burseri', pure white flower; 'Kerneri', yellow; and 'Rhaeticum', orange-yellow.

Petrophytum

Gardeners preferring truly slow-growing dwarf rock plants almost instinctively choose *P. caespitosum*. This shrublike plant likes a sunny location in a trough or the cracks of a rock formation—but only if the substrate drains rapidly. Eventually, it knits dense foliage mats between and over the rocks. During the summer, these mats are decorated with delicate, yellowish flower clusters.

Petrorhagia

The Double-blooming Pink, *P. saxifraga* (syn. *Tunica saxifraga*) 'Plena', is a rock plant with many virtues. It bears charming flowers throughout the summer and well into autumn. Similar in appearance to Baby's Breath, these plants are very durable and prefer sunny locations. *Petrorhagia* should not be absent from any alpine collection. Its long flowering season and the decorative, fragrant flowers make this plant particularly valuable.

Phlox

Clumps of *P. subulata* are essential for their flowers in any rock garden, and several *Phlox* species are suitable for alpine gardens, particularly the highly regarded *P. douglasii* with its dense clumps. Two of its best forms are 'Hybrida' with numerous lilac-pink flowers, and 'Eva' which produces lovely pink flowers, each with a dark eye.

Physoplexis

The dream of every alpine collector is to grow a plant of *P. comosa* (syn. *Phyteuma comosum*), the "Devil's Claw" as it is known in the Dolomite Alps. In early summer the large, almost stemless, upright flower clusters rise over small foliage cushions. The shape of these flowers is clawlike, hence the common local name. Its flower color varies from bluish white at the petal edge to dark purple at the base. Planted in partial shade between rocks, this plant enjoys Basic Mix A, to which a goodly amount of coarse aggregate must be added to improve aeration.

Phyteuma

Two *Phyteuma* species are suitable for the rock garden. Both thrive with little care and few problems. *Phyteuma scheuchzeri* bears vibrant blue, ball-shaped flower clusters on short stems in the spring; *P. sieberi* blooms a bit lighter and remains quite dwarf.

Phyteuma comosum see Physoplexis

Plantago (Plantain)

In contrast with dark rock, *P. nivalis'* silvery white, woolly leaf rosettes look particularly attractive. This attractive plant grows with few worries, so long as it is protected from too much moisture during the winter.

Polygala

Polygala chamaebuxus is a pretty, low shrublet that thrives especially well in warm locations with some mid-day shade. This species flowers readily in yellow with small red spots. More vigorous and hardier is the purple-red flowering form 'Grandiflora'. *Polygala vayredae* can be recommended only for the lover of alpines. It is very susceptible to hard frosts during winter and is likewise sensitive to excess moisture. The flower color of this species is pink with yellow splashes.

Potentilla (Cinquefoil)

The low *Potentilla* species have become essential wherever green carpets are required between rock formations. *Potentilla nitida*—the pink-flowering jewel from the Dolomites—is a lazy bloomer at lower elevations, but there are several later-flowering cultivars. Most of the low-growing *Potentilla* species are grown for the beauty of their foliage alone. In addition to the species mentioned in the earlier section, consider the following: *P. fragiformis* with low, large yellow flowers in early summer; *P. speciosa* with beautiful, silvery white mats; *P. crantzii* with very rich, enduring yellow flower display; and—similar to it—*P. clusiana* with dwarf foliage.

Primula (Primrose)

This very wide-ranging and varied genus contains any number of true treasures for troughs and alpine miniature gardens. For the former, we have the alpine rock primulas, all of which prefer some shade and Basic Mix A, and thrive in rock crevices and narrow cracks.

Lovely golden yellow blooms are

displayed by the true primrose of the Alps, *Primula auricula. P. auricula* var. *albocincta* sports a flour-white dusting on its leaves, as well as bright yellow edges. *Primula clusiana* is one of the most satisfying of the rock-loving primroses; in spring, purple-pink blossoms with lighter-colored throats rise over green foliage rosettes. *Primula wulfenia*, also a copious bloomer, has small, compact leaf rosettes and dark lilac-pink flowers. *Primula spectabilis* is purple-pink and flowers somewhat later. As the name suggests, *P. hirsuta* bears somewhat hairy leaves together with carmine-pink blossoms. Let me also single out *P. marginata* from among the large contingent of alpine primulas. It grows relatively well and is hardy; its lilac flowers appear early in spring. The beautiful and very decorative leaf rosettes are made up of toothed, yellowish powdered foliage. There are several good cultivars of this species, for example, 'Amethyst' with violet-blue blossoms; 'Drakes Form', lavender; and 'Ramona', violet-purple.

Among the Asian primroses, several additional interesting and very beautiful species deserve mention. The most unusual flower is that of *P. vialii*. During the summer, it displays its dense spikes over the foliage when grown in partial shade and moist soil. The flower spike first turns scarlet-red, but the individual blossoms are lilac-colored. Also a lover of wetter sites is *P. farinosa*, the Birdseye Primrose. This one does well in Basic Mix A, but prefers a mixture of the substrates A and D even more. As with almost all *Primula* species, make certain that the plants are not overly wet in winter. Late in summer, the dark lilac-blue flower whorls of *P. capitata* ssp. *mooreana* appear. This subspecies prefers conditions similar to *P. vialii* and looks its best when planted among light-colored rocks.

Primula auricula, the Alpine Primrose, is decorated in May with golden blooms.

Pulsatilla vulgaris blooms early in spring.

117

Pterocephalus

In sunny and dry locations, *P. perennis* ssp. *perennis* (syn. *P. parnassii*) forms dense, light gray-green mats; the pink-colored *Scabiosa*-like blossoms rise from the foliage during summer. This late flowering period makes the plant particularly valuable.

Ptilotrichum

Ptilotrichum spinosum is dense and spikey; white blossoms appear on these shrublets early in summer. Once naturalized, the plant is able to withstand much heat and drought. Even prettier is *P. spinosum* 'Rubrum' with wine-pink blossoms.

Pulsatilla (European Pasque Flower)

The dark violet flowers of *P. vulgaris* (syn. *Anemone pulsatilla*) appear in early spring, emerging from hairy buds. There are hybrids and forms in the most varied colors from dark purple through red to white. All do well in Basic Mix A as long as they are given a sunny site. Somewhat difficult to cultivate is the sulphur-yellow Alpine Anemone, *P. alpina*, (syn. *Anemone alpina*) 'Sulphurea'. It prefers to grow in alpine troughs or rock gardens with Basic Mix B and light shade.

Ramonda

The huge, evergreen, woolly-leafed rosettes are always a decorative element in shaded troughs or in the shade of alpine gardens. Decorated with violet-blue flowers in early summer, *R. myconi* also has forms with pink and white flowers. *Ramonda nathaliae* blooms a bit earlier, with lavender flowers highlighted by orange centers. Once properly naturalized, these *Ramonda* species can withstand long drought periods—provided that they are located in a shady site with humus-rich Basic Mix A soil, amended with peatmoss or Basic Mix D.

Ranunculus

Sunny locations are perfect for *R. gramineus*; this is a tidy species with narrow leaves and bright yellow flowers late in spring. *Ranunculus alpestris*, the Alpine Buttercup, is a treat for collectors of alpine plants and highly recommended. These species prefer some shade with quick-draining Basic Mix A. Large, white flowers on short stems appear in spring over shiny green leaves. The yellow-flowering *R. montanus* is a bit taller and flowers from late spring well into summer, particularly when planted in

(68) A magnificent burst of flowers emerges from this trough containing summer-flowering species. Such special displays may be carefully planned to produce such an effect. *(69)* The unusual *Larix kaempferi,* in the foreground of the alpine trough, forces the viewer to contemplate it in greater detail. Its bizarre form determines the feeling of the design. *(70)* The plants ooze out of this rough-hewn trough as if growing directly out of a rock: Dwarf Broom, *Cytisus decumbens,* with counterpart *Achillea chrysocoma,* and between them a primrose of the Auricula Section, *Primula* × *pubescens,* as well as *Sedum acre* and a Pillow Phlox, *Phlox douglasii.*

light shade with a constant source of moisture. Strictly a plant collector's species is *R. glacialis*, a jewel among the alpine plants. If planted in moist soil mixed well with a large quantity of gravel, this species will thrive. It repays careful care with large white flowers tinted in shades from light to dark pink. Use Basic Mix B mixed with Basic Mix D at the sub-soil level. The surface must be topdressed with coarse gravel and rock chips.

Raoulia

Flat, thick, silvery white foliage carpets are the mark of *R. hookeri* (syn. *R. australis*). It thrives in sunny sites between rocks and prefers protection from winter moisture. Just as flat-growing are the mats of *R. tenuicaulis;* however, they are a bit less dense and not quite as silvery white. This species is less susceptible to excess moisture. *Raoulia glabra* is covered in summer with dense, green mats and silvery haired blossoms. The lovely dwarf *R. lutescens* weaves small, dense, grayish green dwarf mats when planted in Basic Mix B between adjoining rocks.

Rosularia

Rosularia persica is an unusual rosette plant with some characteristics of *Sempervivum*, notably its meaty, narrow, green leaf rosettes with reddish tips. If the rosettes are protected from winter moisture, the plants fare very well in Basic Mix A and are particularly attractive between rocks and in perforated limestone.

Saponaria

Gorgeous, flat, dense green mats are the hallmark of *S.* × *olivana*. It is also distinguished by a mass of large, almost erect, reddish pink blooms. This species is well suited for planting in a limestone rock but will do just as well when planted in crevices. Not long after planting, the foliage will spill out of the smallest of crevices. Lovely, intensely dark pink blossoms decorate 'Bressingham Glow', which is also noted for its very dense mats. Collectors of alpines should also consider *S.* × *wiemannii*, which is similar to *S. olivana* and blooms pink, as well as *S. lutea* with light yellow blossoms. Because *S. cypria* flowers almost the entire summer, this species is very popular. Though its mats are loose, the growth is very bushy, and it flowers gladly with large, dark reddish pink blossoms. Some protection from winter moisture is recommended.

Saxifraga (Saxifrage)

A genus with many different species, cultivars and forms, *Saxifraga* excites the lover of alpine plants but also enriches any miniature rock garden. The forms of *S. rosacea* are essential to any alpine garden. Its rosettes are densely formed, often coated with lime, stiff, and attractive-looking all year round. But planted between rocks in sunny to partially shaded sites, these rosette plants are particularly attractive when planted in the holes of perforated limestone.

Saxifraga paniculata (syn. *S. aizoon*), decorated in late spring with white flower clusters, has smaller, more densely arrayed rosettes. There are many cultivars, such as 'Lutea', creamy yellow; 'Multipunctata', white spotted red; 'Baldensis', small, dense rosettes; and 'Minutifolia', known for its tiny rosettes.

Saxifraga callosa (syn. *S. lingulata*) has gorgeous white flower panicles on mostly brown flower stalks rising from narrow, spade-shaped leaves. Several of its better forms are: 'Superba', its dark brown stems making a beautiful contrast to its white flowers; 'Latonica' with red-spotted flowers; and 'Bellardi' with very narrow elongated rosettes.

Large rosettes with wide, spatula-shaped leaves are developed by *S. cotyledon* 'Pyramidalis'. Its large white flower truss is a special point of interest during the blooming period in late spring.

The king of the saxifrages is *S. longifolia*. Unfortunately, true forms of this plant are difficult to find, since it does not form offsets so can only be propagated from seed. By crossing it with other *Saxifraga* species, a number of similar forms appear that are no less beautiful, but the true form can only be raised from certified seed. The rosette of *S. longifolia*, a narrow-leaved semiglobe of severe beauty, can develop to considerable size: 8–12 in. wide (20–30 cm) rosettes are not at all rare. A lovely flower cluster that often branches back to the base completes the image of this truly regal species. *Saxifraga longifolia* grows well in east-facing crevices and in the holes of perforated limestone or tufa.

Some of the earliest are the spring-flowering saxifrages of the Kabschia or Engleria sections. These very dwarf, clump-forming species develop best in areas with some shade, preferably facing east to north in rock crevices, and in tufa and perforated limestone. They are also well suited for planters and window boxes, as long as they get some shade. They are always small treasures when they spread their evergreen, compact tufts and send out their graceful flower spikes. The most satisfactory species and cultivars are found among the yellow-flowering representatives of the Kabschia Section: *S. apiculata*, undemanding, with heavy bloom and steady growth; *S. sancta*, which has very dense, stiff rosettes and blooms much like the similarly very hardy *S. × haagii*; and *S. franzii* with its numerous, light yellow flowers. The recent introduction 'Golden Prague' produces long-lived, orange-yellow flowers.

Of the many species, cultivars and forms that are offered today, let me make special mention of several more: *S. grisebachii* 'Wisley' with red blossoms and particularly large rosettes. Of the white-flowering *S. burseriana* there are several good forms, namely 'Gloria', dark flower stalks; 'Pilatus', sulphur-yellow; and the light yellow 'Sulphurea'. See also 'Cranbourne', lilac-pink blossoms; *S. irwingii*, reddish pink; and the very hardy *S. sempervivum* (syn. *S. porophylla* var. *thessalica*) which has solid red flowers. Anyone fortunate enough to see a boulder of perforated limestone, planted with different species/cultivars of this group in full bloom is, I am sure, totally entranced by the sight. Several such rocks planted on the shady side with Kabschias and on the sunny side with *S. rosacea*, located in the garden or even on a terrace, make for a stunning display! Between the rocks, clumps of mosslike *S. arendsii* cultivars create soft, green mats.

In partly shaded sites between rocks *S. tricuspidata* forms small, dense, dwarf pillows which produce white flowers. Another species preferring some shade is *S. oppositifolia*; use Basic Mix B amended with material for even greater permeability and it will do well, particularly when its loose, creeping tufts have been topdressed with fine gravel. Its large, purplish red flowers appear in spring. There are several good cultivars of this species, including the very flowery 'Splendens'.

For the shady areas between rocks, the *Saxifraga* commonly known as London Pride, *S. umbrosa* 'Elliotts Variety', will prosper and display its delicate, reddish pink flowers. Those who enjoy yellow-marbled foliage will want to plant the form 'Aureo-Punctata'. Late in autumn, *S. cortusifolia* var. *fortunei* flowers in the shade under some protection. Particularly effective are the white flower clusters of the form 'Rubrifolia', which stand over the ruby-red foliage.

Schivereckia

A winter-hardy, pillow-forming genus similar to *Arabis*, *Schivereckia* species are notable for their tiny, dwarf pillows, such as those of *S. bornmuelleri*. In the spring, numerous white blossoms appear over the dense, grayish green foliage pillows. This plant does well in a variety of growing conditions.

Scleranthus

Scleranthus uniflorus has a remarkable brown coloring in its dwarf foliage mat. Beautiful contrasts with the green and gray-green of the remainder of mat-forming plants can be made using this species.

Scutellaria

The low, loose carpets of *S. orientalis* serve as the base for a plant whose flowering period, July–September, recommends it to growers desiring late, long-blooming plants. The yellow, helmet-shaped flowers sit practically upright on the gray, woolly foliage. This species prefers to be kept on the dry side during the winter.

Sedum

Sedum species are essential for any rock garden. Several are suited for alpine miniature gardens and—together with *Sempervivum* and similar plants—they can weave magic when set out among rock formations. Creating entrancing plant scenery is especially easy with *S. spathulifolium*, its cultivars 'Cape Blanco' and 'Purpureum'. The former is very beautiful during bloom in early summer when the silvery white coated fleshy leaflets are set off by the golden flowers. 'Purpureum' is a larger plant; its fleshy leaves are purple with a slight indumentum, and it bears golden yellow flowers. *Sedum nevii* is also attractive; its low, dense rosettes are brownish green, providing a fine base for its white flowers during summer. Bluish green, dense, dwarf pillows made up of tiny, ball-shaped leaflets are the mark of *S. dasyphyllum*, which develops pale pink flowers in the summer. The foliage hugs the rocks and boulders and looks very attractive. Beautiful single rosettes surmounted by red flowers characterize the biannual *S. sempervivoides*, a species that mimics the foliage of *Sempervivum*. After flowering, take seed from this plant, since the rosettes then die; re-seeding is not at all difficult.

Sempervivella

From summer until well into autumn, *S. sedoides* covers its low-growing rosette pillows with white, star-shaped blooms. Provide protection from excess winter moisture. This plant thrives under cover or in an alpine greenhouse.

Sempervivum (Houseleek)

This exceptionally varied genus provides

many little treasures for troughs, slab gardens, and alpine gardens. Apart from the true species, there are a great number of hybrids, most of which produce large, single rosettes. All develop spreading carpets of rosettes from offsets which gradually cover the tightest crevices and shallowest hollows.

Of the voluminous number of plants available, let me highlight several representatives: S. arachnoideum ssp. tomentosum receives its "spidery" name from the delicate silvery web covering its rosettes. There are several good cultivars: 'Minor' with very small single rosettes; or the gorgeous 'Shootrolds Triumph' with dark brownish red, round, silvery webbed rosettes, as well as bright reddish pink blossoms. Sempervivum blandum produces brownish red rosettes on an olive-green base and purple-pink blossoms. Very beautiful, round (almost ball-shaped) rosettes with whitish fuzz are the hallmark of S. ciliosum. The well-known Hen and Chickens (S. tectorum) is also available in many forms, and numerous good garden plants with mostly large rosettes are derived from this species. Let me only mention 'Alpha', reddish brown rosettes and pink blossoms; 'Beta', beautiful, fringed, reddish brown rosettes and dark pink flowers; and 'Rubin' with strong, ruby-red rosettes. Sempervivum calcareum has light green leaf rosettes with dark red-brown tips; the rosettes of its cultivar 'Nocturno' are dark purplish brown, while 'Rheinkiesel' forms dense, silver-webbed rosettes.

Sempervivum heuffelii see *Jovibarba heuffelii*

Senecio

Apart from the summer-flowering, stunning, yellow-blooming S. tiroliensis, S. siegfriedi enlivens an alpine display with its beautiful silvery gray foliage. Similar to these, S. ferdinandi has lighter-colored yellow blossoms, and S. suendermannii a silvery gray foliage.

Silene (Campion)

Gorgeous green, dense, dwarf carpets are typical of S. acaulis. This species is essential in alpine troughs or slab gardens, but is just as useful in planters and window boxes. The native species does not bloom in cultivation as well as it does in the highlands, where the reddish pink blossoms practically cover the foliage, but several perfectly acceptable garden forms exist that do. Consider 'Floribunda', a certain bloomer every year; 'Plena', with its very attractive dark pink, double flowers; 'Correvoniana' also is double, but its blooms are lighter in color. Apart from the different pink-blooming forms, there is also the white-flowering 'Alba'.

All species thrive in sunny or lightly shaded locations, nestled between rocks in rapidly draining soil. For the demanding collector of alpines, I recommend the very dwarf cultivar S. acaulis 'Excapa'. Its reddish pink flowers are virtually stemless, seeming to rest on top of the foliage.

Soldanella

Soldanella blooms with its fringed, lilac bells shortly after snowmelt in the mountains, but is very difficult to raise in a garden setting. Only in shaded and somewhat moist sites growing in Basic Mix D, possibly amended with Basic Mix B, will the lavender-blue-flowering S. montana have a chance of survival. Soldanella alpina is even more delicate, and its lilac-colored, finely fringed bells develop earlier in the year.

Solidago (Goldenrod)

Mid-autumn is the time when the very dwarf and low-creeping, golden yellow *S. minutissima* proves its worth. Barely an inch (2–3 cm) high, the flower plumes reach toward the sun. The late blooming period alone makes this species particularly desirable. It grows easily and also thrives in planters and window boxes.

Talinum

The tiny, mat-forming succulent *T. okanoganense* looks best when placed among *Sempervivum*, *Rosularia*, or *Orostachys*. Its white, funnel-shaped flowers appear in late summer. This species is susceptible to damage from winter moisture, so is well suited for the alpine greenhouse.

Teucrium (Germander)

Teucrium montanum, the summer-flowering Yellow Germander of the Alps, spreads gray, hirsute foliage mats wherever the soil drains quickly. As with all other species of *Teucrium*, it thrives in a sunny location protected from too much moisture during the winter. The pink-blooming *T. mussimonum* produces particularly lovely, gray, woolly prostrate mats formed of rounded leaves. *Teucrium pyrenaicum* blooms during the summer with light yellow blossoms and also forms dense, woolly, dwarf carpets.

Thalictrum (Meadow Rue)

The representatives of this genus are almost all very interesting, shade-loving shrubs for larger displays. The only true dwarf, *T. kiusianum*, is of Japanese origin, remains low-growing and in summer opens feathery, lilac flower clusters. This dwarf species grows best in humus-enriched soil (try Basic Mix D or A mixed with peatmoss) and also prefers some shade.

Thlaspi

Thlaspi montanum, the most robust representative of this genus, decorates its dense leaf pillows in spring with low, white flower clusters. *Thlaspi rotundifolium* requires considerably more attention in planting and tending. A planting medium of a base made with Basic Mix B topped by coarser materials for better aeration and drainage is preferred. The surface should be topdressed with fine gravel. Between these stone chips the rosettelike pillows arise; in late spring expect violet flowers. The same cultural demands are made by *T. stylosum*, which opens its lilac blooms early in the year over dwarf foliage. Both species must be protected from winter moisture and placed in semishade. During periods of active growth, they cannot be allowed to dry out.

Townsendia

Attractive plants, particularly for miniature rock gardens, troughs, and planters, this genus from the mountainous regions of North America has much to offer. In the case of *T. formosa* and *T. grandiflora*, the asterlike, violet or purple flowers arise on short stems and bloom early in the summer over narrow leafed rosettes. *Townsendia parryi* displays its large, lilac flowers during summer—as well as its coarse appearing stem. *Townsendia wilcoxiana* produces very short-stemmed, violet flowers with a large central disk; the flowers rise in summer over spatula-shaped, leaf rosettes. The tiniest dwarf is *T. rothrockii*. Its lilac-pink "aster flowers" are almost stemless as they float just over the leaf rosettes. All these species require protection from winter moisture and usually have a short lifespan. However, it is worth the effort to replace these lovely denizens of the rockery by re-seeding.

Trachelium

A welcome summer color is produced by *T. jacquinii* (syn. *T. rumelianum*) with its lilac-blue bloom. This undemanding plant enjoys placing its new shoots directly on the rockface.

Trollius (Globeflower)

Trollius pumilus—the low-growing, yellow-flowering, dwarf species—is well-suited for cultivation in shaded troughs or moister areas of the rock garden. The cupped flowers appear early in summer on short stems.

Tunica see *Petrorhagia*

Valeriana

Valeriana supina decorates its lovely, green, dwarf pillows with lilac-pink flower clusters during early summer. Somewhat shorter are the red blooms of *V. suendermannii*. Both species thrive in sunny sites. *V. celtica* demands a very humus-rich soil—a sandy Basic Mix D works well. It also prefers some shade, so east-facing or north planting sites are best.

Verbascum (Mullein)

Of all the verbascum species, only *V. dumulosum* can be recommended for miniature gardens. Its ideal environment is the alpine greenhouse or a trough with some overhead cover, so that moisture can be better regulated. A moisture-free growing area during winter and a sunny, warm location at other times is essential for good growth. In summer the large, yellow flowers appear in great number on the low, gray, hirsute plants.

Veronica (Speedwell)

Within this variable genus a goodly number of dwarf alpine forms exist, all of which are well suited for planting in alpine miniature gardens. *Veronica armena* is a heavily flowering and especially hardy species. Like its reddish pink cultivar 'Rosea', it blooms in spring but with a violet flower. *Veronica satureioides* squeezes its loose, evergreen carpet into the rock, and its azure-blue flowers burst forth early in summer. Like its parent, the form 'Kellereri' produces shiny green and very dense pillows. What a beautiful image as the foliage spreads over a trough or a rock! *Veronica schmidtiana*, a summer-flowering (blue) species, forms beautiful, flat leaf mats.

Veronica caespitosa thoroughly enjoys growing in narrow cracks—and, if possible, even more so in the holes of perforated limestone or tufa. From such confined spaces, it sends out dense, dwarf clumps of woolly leaves. The bright blue, almost upright flowers appear early in spring. The prerequisite for good growth of these plants is a well-drained, permeable soil (Basic Mix B) that quickly drains winter moisture. These *Veronica* species develop their full beauty in the alpine greenhouse.

Veronica bonarota see *Paederota*

Vitaliana

Among the rocks, *V. primuliflora* ssp. *praetutiana* (syn. *Douglasia vitaliana* ssp. *praetutiana*) spreads out its dense, solid, silvery gray foliage. In late spring, yellow blossoms appear above them. Its cultivar 'Tridentata' has green foliage, while that of 'Gaudinii' is a solid, grayish green. All prefer the permeable soil of Basic Mix A or B.

Wulfenia

Apart from *W. carinthiaca,* the more delicate *W. baldacii* and *W. amherstiana* can be recommended. *Wulfenia* × *suendermannii* is notable for its rich bloom. All share violet-blue flowers, a cluster habit, and a preference for shady sites in humus-enriched but permeable soil.

Grasses and Sedges

While grasses in larger rock gardens "loosen" the appearance of a plant collection and so provide a special accent in the design, few grasses can be recommended for alpine miniature gardens. Try *Festuca glauca*—or better yet, the slower-growing *F. valesiaca* 'Glaucantha'—in window boxes or planters dominated by several dwarf conifers. In true alpine gardens, only a handful of dwarf-growing species that do not become a bother (due to vigorous growth or an abundance of seeds) are suitable.

Alopecurus lanatus possesses white, hirsute leaves enhanced by a woolly appearance. *Carex firma* forms small, dense, green clumps among alpine plants. *Carex ornithopoda* does not remain small for long; however, the cultivar 'Variegata' is attractive, thanks to its whitish, variegated, narrow leaves. *Poa alpina,* the Alpine Bluegrass (and particularly its subspecies *vivipara*), is an elegant and interesting form, since young plants appear at the tips of the seed heads. Most other species grow too quickly for use in miniature gardens and are best reserved for planting in larger landscapes.

Ferns

Among the ferns there are several dwarf forms that can be recommended for planting in the shadier areas of a miniature garden. Be it a window box in the shade, a shaded trough, or the partially shaded side of a rock garden, these small ferns thrive in Basic Mix A amended with additional peat moss.

Asplenium ruta-muraria is comfortable in both shaded and sunny locations between rocks and in crevices. The dark green year-round fronds are always effective. *Blechnum spicant* usually creates flat rosettes with its evergreen fronds. *Ceterach officinarum* likes sunny cracks and can handle fairly long periods of drought once established. The tasseled fronds of *Cystopteris fragilis* flourish in shaded rock formations. Also very useful are the many forms of Hart's Tongue Fern, *Phyllitis scolopendrium,* all of which share the basic traits of leathery, evergreen foliage and a preference for moist locations. *Polypodium vulgare,* commonly called Angel Sweet, prefers Basic Mix D and bears evergreen, tasseled fronds. Of the genus *Polystichum,* noted for its height, *P. lonchitis* can be recommended for use in a miniature garden. It has dark green, stiff, simple fronds which remain green throughout the year.

Selection Guide

The following guides which provide a summary of the plants described in this chapter are divided into three categories: rock garden species, alpine plants, and rock plants. These terms also indicate their landscape use. The lists summarize the plants in each category so the gardener may use them to select the plants best suited for his landscape objectives and feel a sense of surety in gathering a collection of plants. Species and varieties particularly recommended are indicated by an asterisk (*).

Rock Garden Perennials Notable for Their Flower Displays

Acaena buchananii
– microphylla
Alyssum montanum 'Berggold'
– saxatile
— 'Citrinum'
— 'Compactum'*
— 'Dudley Neville'*
— 'Plenum'
Androsace primuloides
Antennaria tomentosa hort. (syn. *A. dioica* var. *borealis*)
– dioica var. *borealis*
— 'Nywood'
— 'Rubra'
Arabis caucasica 'Plena'
— 'Schneehaube'
Armeria maritima 'Düsseldorfer Stolz'
Aster alpinus
– dumosus 'Nesthäkchen'*
Aubrieta hybrids*

Campanula carpatica cultivars
– poscharskyana 'Blauranke'*
Carlina acaulis

Cerastium tomentosum var. *columnae**
Chrysogonum virginianum

Dianthus allwoodi
– caesius (syn. *D. gratianopolitanus*)
*– gratianopolitanus** and cultivars

*Euphorbia myrsinites**

Gentiana acaulis 'Dinarica'
– septemfida var. *lagodechiana**
Gypsophila repens 'Rosenschleier'

Helianthemum chamaecistus (syn. *H. nummularium*)
– nummularium
— 'Zonatus'*
– 'Sterntaler'
Heliosperma alpestre (syn. *Silene alpestris*)

Iberis saxatilis
– sempervirens
Inula ensifolia 'Compacta'

*Minuartia laricifolia**

Oenothera missouriensis

Phlox subulata cultivars*
Potentilla aurea 'Goldklumpen'
— ssp. *chrysocraspeda*
– ternata (syn. *P. aurea* ssp. *chrysocraspeda*)

Saponaria ocymoides
Saxifraga-Arendsii hybrids
– hypnoides var. *egemmulosa**
– muscoides 'Findling'
Sedum cauticolum
– floriferum 'Weihenstephaner Gold'*
– kamtschaticum 'Fol. Var.'
– spurium 'Coccineum'*
Sempervivum, all species and cultivars producing large rosettes*
Silene alpestris 'Pleniflorum'*
– schafta 'Splendens'*

Thymus praecox var. *pseudolanuginosus**

– pseudolanuginosus (syn. *T. praecox* var. *lanuginosus*)
– serpyllum 'Coccineum'

Veronica prostrata
— 'Alba'

Wulfenia carinthiaca

Alpine Plants

Dependable and resilient species and cultivars for alpine planters, window boxes, trough gardens and similar containers.

For sunny locations and doing best in Basic Mix A.

Achillea ageratifolia
*– × kellereri**
– wilczeckii
Aëthionema grandiflorum
– warleyense
— 'Warley Rose'*
— 'Warley Rubrum'*
Alopecurus lanatus
*Alyssum moellendorfianum**
– montanum 'Berggold'
Anacyclus depressus
Androsace primuloides
– sarmentosa and all its cultivars
*– sempervivoides**
Andryala agardhii
Anemone × lesseri
– narcissiflora
*Anthemis biebersteiniana**
Arabis androsacea
– scopoliana
*Arenaria ledebouriana**
– montana 'Grandiflora'
– tetraquetra
Armeria caespitosa (syn. *A. juniperifolia*)
*– juniperifolia**
– suendermannii
Artemisia schmidtiana 'Nana'*

Asperula cynanchica
– lilaciflora 'Caespitosa'*
Asplenium ruta-muraria
Aster natalense
Azorella trifurcata

Callianthemum anemonoides
– coriandrifolium
*Campanula cochleariifolia**
– garganica
– portenschlagiana 'Birch Hybrid'*
– pusilla (syn. *C. cochleariifolia*)
Carex firma
– ornithopoda
— 'Variegata'
Ceterach officinarum
*Chrysanthemum weyrichii**
Codonopsis clematidea
– meleagris
– ovata
Cymbalaria muralis 'Globosa Rosea'

Dianthus alpinus
– arenarius
– gratianopolitanus 'Blaureif'*
— 'Compactus'*
– 'La Bourbrille'
– neglectus (syn. *D. pavonicus*)
– noeanus (syn. *D. petraeus* ssp. *noeanus*)
– pavonicus
– petraeus ssp. *noeanus**
*– simulans**
– sylvestris
Dodecatheon meadia
– pauciflorum (syn. *D. meadia*)
– 'Red Wings'
Douglasia (syn. *Vitaliana*)
Draba aizoides
*– bruniifolia**
— var. *diversifolia**
– lasiocarpa
– olympica hort. (syn. *D. bruniifolia* (Sibth.) non hort.)*
– suendermannii

Dryas drummondii
– *octopetala*
– × *suendermannii**

*Edraianthus dinaricus**
– *graminifolius*
– *tenuifolius*
Erigeron aurantiacus
– *leiomerus**
Erinus alpinus 'Albus'
— 'Dr. Hähnle'*
Eriogonum jamesii
– *racemosum*
– *umbellatum*
Euphorbia capitulata
Euryops evansii

Festuca glauca
– *valesiaca* 'Glaucantha'

Galium baldense
Gentiana acaulis and its cultivars
– *decumbens*
– *kurroo*
– *septemfida* 'Doeringiana'*
— 'Erecta'
Geranium cinereum 'Ballerina'
– *dalmaticum*
— 'Album'
– *subcaulescens* 'Splendens'*
*Geum montanum**
*Globularia cordifolia**
– *lindavica*
Gymnandra (syn. *Lagotis*)
Gypsophila cerastioides
– *tenuifolia**

Helianthemum alpestre (syn. *H. oelandicum* ssp. *alpestre*)
– *canum*
– *oelandicum**
H. oelandicum ssp. *alpestre*
— 'Serpyllifolium'
– *scardicum*
Hieracium bombycinum

– *villosum**
*Hippocrepis comosa**
Hutchinsia alpina
— ssp. *auerswaldii*
– *auerswaldii* (syn. *H. alpina* ssp. *auerswaldii*)

*Iberis saxatilis**
Incarvillea mairei and its cultivars
*Iris cristata**
– *danfordiae*
– *lacustris**
– *reticulata*

Jovibarba heuffelii

Lagotis stolonifera
Leontopodium alpinum and its cultivars
– *himalayanum*
– *palibinianum*
– *souliei**
— 'Mignon'*
– *stracheyi*
Linaria alpina
— 'Rosea'
– *cymbalaria* (syn. *Cymbalaria*)
Linum alpinum (syn. *L. perenne* ssp. *alpinum*)
– *perenne* ssp. *alpinum**
Lotus corniculatus 'Plenus'*

Marrubium supinum
Micromeria croatica
– *microphylla*
Minuartia graminifolia
– *laricifolia**
Moltkia × *intermedia*
– *petraea*

Ononis cenisia (syn. *O. cristata*)
– *cristata*
*Onosma albo-rosea**
– *stellulata*
Orostachys spinosus

Papaver alpinum

Petrophytum caespitosum*
Petrorhagia saxifraga
— 'Plena'
Phlox douglasii
— 'Eva'
— 'Hybrida'*
Phyteuma scheuchzeri
– *sieberi*
Plantago nivalis*
Poa alpina var. *vivipara*
Potentilla clusiana
– *crantzii*
– *fragiformis**
– *nitida*
– *speciosa*
Pterocephalus parnassii (syn. *P. perennis*
   ssp. *perennis*)
– *perennis* ssp. *perennis*
Ptilotrichum spinosum
— 'Rubrum'
Pulsatilla vulgaris and its cultivars

Ranunculus gramineus
Raoulia glabra*
– *tenuicaulis*
Rosularia persica

Saponaria 'Bressingham Glow'
– *cypria*
– × *olivana*
– × *wiemannii*
Saxifraga aizoon (syn. *S. paniculata*)
– *callosa** and its cultivars
– *cotyledon* 'Pyramidalis'*
– *lingulata* (syn. *S. callosa*)
– *paniculata* and its cultivars*
– *tricuspidata*
Schivereckia bornmuelleri
Scutellaria orientalis
Sedum dasphyllum
– *nevii*
– *spathulifolium*
— 'Cape Blanco'*
— 'Purpureum'*

Sempervivella sedoides
Sempervivum, all species and cultivars
   producing small rosettes
– *heuffelii* (syn. *Jovibarba heuffelii*)
Senecio tiroliensis
Silene acaulis and its cultivars*
Solidago minutissima

Teucrium montanum
Thlaspi montanum
Townsendia formosa
– *grandiflora*
Trachelium jacquinii
– *rumelianum* (syn. *T. jacquinii*)
Tunica (syn. *Petrorhagia*)

Valeriana × *suendermannii*
– *supina*
Veronica armena
— 'Rosea'*
– *satureioides*
— 'Kellereri'*
– *schmidtiana**
Vitaliana primuliflora ssp. *praetutiana*
— 'Tridentata'
— 'Gaudinii'

For shady areas, and doing best in Basic
Mix A amended with peat moss.

Aquilegia akitensis (syn. *A. flabellata*)
– *caerulea* 'Biedermeier'*
– *canadensis*
– *einseleana*
– *flabellata* 'Mini Star'
— 'Nana'
– *glandulosa*
Asplenium ruta-muraria
– *trichomanes*

Blechnum spicant

Campanula cochleariifolia*
– *garganica*
– *portenschlagiana* 'Birch Hybrid'*

– *pusilla* (syn. *C. cochleariifolia*)
Ceterach officinarum
Chiastophyllum oppositifolium
Cyclamen europaeum (syn. *C.*
    purpurascens)
– *hederifolium*
– *linearifolium* (syn. *C. hederifolium*)
– *neapolitanum* (syn. *C. hederifolium*)
– *purpurascens*
Cystopteris fragilis

Gentiana farreri
– × *macaulayi* and all its forms*
– *sino-ornata*

Haberlea rhodopensis
— 'Viminalis'
Horminum pyrenaicum*

Mentha requienii

Nierembergia repens

Phyllitis scolopendrium and its cultivars
Polypodium vulgare
Polystichum lonchitis
Primula auricula*
— var. *albo-cincta*
– *clusiana**
– *spectabilis*
– *vialii*
– *wulfeniana*

Ramonda myconi
– *nathaliae*

Saxifraga cortusifolia var. *fortunei*
— 'Rubrifolia'
Saxifraga umbrosa 'Aureo-Punctata'*
— 'Elliot's Variety'*
Soldanella montana

Trollius pumilus

Wulfenia amherstiana
– *baldaccii*
– × *suendermannii*

Rock Plants

These require good culture and conscientious attention to the guidelines provided in the chapter on cultivation.

For sunny or bright/lightly shaded sites. The majority require Basic Mix B or sandy Basic Mix A, amended with pumice or similar material.

Acantholimon glumaceum*
– *graminifolium*
– *olivieri*
Achillea clavennae
– *umbellata*
Aethionema oppositifolium
Androsace chamaejasme
– *foliosa*
– *helvetica*
– *imbricata*
– *lanuginosa* 'Leichtlinii'*
– *pyrenaica**
– *strigillosa*
– *villosa**
— var. *arachnoidea*
Anemone alpina (syn. *Pulsatilla alpina*)
Anthemis barrelieri
Arabis pumila
– *vochinensis*
Arenaria purpurascens
– *sajanensis*
Artemisia assoana
– *laxa* (syn. *A. umbelliformis*)
– *nitida*
– *umbelliformis**
Asperula arcadiensis*
– *nitida**
– *pontica*
Astragalus angustifolius*
– *monspessulanus*

Chrysanthemum alpinum

Dianthus microlepis*

*– musalae**
Draba mollissima
– polytricha

*Edraianthus pumilio**
– serpyllifolius
— 'Albo-Violacea'
Erigeron radicatus
Erodium chamaedryoides (syn. *E. reichardii*)
– cheilanthifolium (syn. *E. petraeum* ssp. *crispum*)
– chrysanthum
– petraeum ssp. *crispum**
– reichardii
— 'Plenum'
— 'Roseum'
– sibthorpianum

Galium incanum
– olympicum
Gentiana bavarica
– verna
Globularia nana (syn. *G. repens*)
– repens
*Gypsophila aretioides**
— 'Caucasica'

Helianthemum lunulatum
Helichrysum frigidum
*– milfordiae**
– sibthorpii
– virgineum (syn *H. sibthorpii*)

Iberis candolleana
– pygmaea
Incarvillea mairei 'Bees Pink'
— 'Frank Rudlow'
— 'Nyoto Sama'
Iris japonica

Leontopodium alpinum
— 'Alpengarten'*
— vera*
Lewisia cotyledon and its cultivars

— var. *howellii*
*– heckneri**
– nevadense
– rediviva
– tweedyi
Linum capitatum
– viscosum

Meconopsis betonicifolia
– horridula
– napaulensis
– paniculata
Minuartia subnivalis

Opuntia humifusa
– phaecantha var. *camanchica*
– rhodantha
Origanum amanum
*– laevigatum**

Paederota bonarota
Papaver alpinum and cultivars
Physoplexis comosa
Phyteuma (syn. *Physoplexis*)
Polygala chamaebuxus
— 'Grandiflora'*
– vayredae
Pulsatilla alpina
— 'Sulphurea'

Ranunculus alpestris
– glacialis
*– montanus**
Raoulia australis (syn. *R. hookeri*)
*– hookeri**
– lutescens

Saponaria lutea
Saxifraga longifolia
Scleranthus uniflorus
Sedum sempervivoides
Senecio ferdinandi
– siegfriedi
– suendermannii
Soldanella alpina

Talinum okanoganense
Teucrium mussimonum
– pyrenaicum
Thalictrum kiusianum
Townsendia parryi
– rothrockii
wilcoxiana

Valeriana celtica
Verbascum dumulosum
Veronica bonarota (syn. *Paederota*
    bonarota)
– caespitosa

For shady site, Basic Mix B.

Calceolaria biflora
– polyrrhiza
*Campanula cashmiriana**
– excisa
– morettiana
– zoysii
Cyclamen coum
— 'Album'

Primula capitata ssp. *mooreana*
– farinosa
– hirsuta
– marginata and its cultivars*

Saxifraga × *apiculata**
– burseriana
Saxifraga burseriana and its cultivars
– franzii
– 'Golden Prague'
– grisebachii 'Wisley'
– × *haagii**
– irwingii
– oppositifolia
— 'Splendens'
– porophylla var. *thessalica* (syn. *S.*
    sempervivum)
*– sancta**
– sempervivum

Thlaspi rotundifolium
– stylosum

Planting Models for Containers, Window Boxes and Troughs

The several examples provided here are suggested not only as intrinsically interesting landscapes, but also to stimulate the reader's imagination as to how troughs, window boxes and containers might be planted. Obviously, all these examples can be modified and adapted to the needs and tastes of the individual gardener. What is most important is finding the proper

The dominant element in this planter is—apart from several interesting rocks—the dwarf spruce, *Picea glauca* 'Laurin'. On the south-facing side (front) a small, dwarf broom (*Genista villarsii*) drapes its branches over the side, as does the long-blooming (late summer until well into autumn) *Sedum sieboldii*. In between, the spring-flowering Stemless Gentian, *G. acaulis* 'Dinarica', creates green clumps; in front of the spruce, the profusely flowering spring blooms of low-growing Edelweiss, *Leontopodium alpinum* 'Alpengarten', decorate the surface with white stars. At the edge *Silene acaulis* 'Floribunda', a heavy-flowering cultivar of Campion, creates a dense, green, dwarf cushion. *Potentilla argyrophylla*—an interesting foliage plant from the Himalayas—adds decoration. Next to it, *Petrorhagia saxifraga* 'Plena' blooms all summer, displaying its dainty, reddish pink blossoms.

Between the rocks and the dense, upright structure of the source a harmonic, but perhaps also a bit severe, relationship exists which is given a special charm by the light-hearted effect of the looser-growing companions.

The dwarf juniper, *Juniperus squamata* 'Loderi', provides the background in this planter. Almost in the center, next to several interesting rocks, the very large, reddish green rosettes of *Sempervivum* 'Sponnier' creep at the rocks' base. The gray mats of *Helianthemum scardicum* drape over the edge. On the opposite side, *Globularia cordifolia* spreads its cushion over the edge, while in the foreground a Rock Pink, *Dianthus simulans*, forms dense clumps.

The restriction to a few species, though several plants of each, provides a peaceful design. The beautiful shapes of the rocks are thereby permitted to make themselves felt.

harmonious relationship between trees and shrubs and alpine perennials. These models were not created while sitting at a conference table, but rather have grown out of practical experience. They have passed the acid test of having endured for years in the Alpine Garden at Pforzheim, West Germany.

Their natural character is established almost exclusively with rocks, including tall formations, or root stumps. These latter elements are not specifically marked in the following sketches.

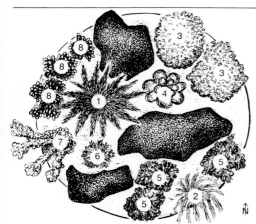

Planter in sunny location with Basic Mix A. Diameter 16 in. (40 cm); depth 5–6 in. (12–14 cm).

1. *Picea glauca* 'Laurin'
2. *Genista villarsii*
3. *Petrorhagia saxifraga* (syn. *Tunica saxifraga*) 'Plena'
4. *Potentilla argyrophylla*
5. *Gentiana acaulis* 'Dinarica'
6. *Leontopodium alpinum* 'Alpengarten'
7. *Sedum sieboldii*
8. *Silene acaulis* 'Floribunda'

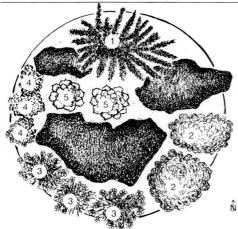

Planter in sunny location. Basic Mix A; diameter 16 in. (40 cm); depth 6 in. (15 cm).

1. *Juniperus squamata* 'Loderi'
2. *Helianthemum scardicum*
3. *Dianthus simulans*
4. *Globularia cordifolia*
5. *Sempervivum* 'Sponnier'

135

The design of this planter depends upon the inclusion of several very impressive rocks. Between them the dwarf *Picea glauca* 'Echiniformis' creates a low-growing, globular, blue-needled ball. A green dwarf juniper, *Juniperus sabina* 'Skandia', spreads over the front edge, as does the dark green, dwarf cushion of *Helianthemum oelandicum*, an early summer-flowering species, next to it. Between the rocks and the edge, the silvery white rosettes of *Saxifraga paniculata* grow with the distinctive, red-dotted flower form of 'Balcana'. The very dense, dwarf pillows of *Vitaliana primuliflora* 'Tridentata' are also sited between the rock and the edge; they are decorated in spring with golden flowers. On the opposite side, *Veronica satureioides* 'Kelleri' drapes its green mat over the edge, and later in the spring the new shoots are covered with blue flowers. Next to it, *Sempervivella sedoides* spreads, and *Erinus alpinus* 'Dr. Hähnle' shows off its small carmine-red flower clusters during the spring blooming period. Along the upper (back) edge, the *Edraianthus tenuifolius* sends its stemmed blue flower clusters in late spring over the side of the planter.

The special element in this planter is the dwarf blue juniper, *Juniperus squamata* 'Blue Star', planted along the edge. This plant should be a mature specimen but preferably of an uneven habit; the more gnarled the better. In front of the juniper and between the rocks, *Saxifraga callosa* 'Superba' forms its narrow-leafed, silvery rosettes decorated in the spring with lovely white panicles. In the foreground between the rock and the edge, the Rock Pink, *Dianthus* 'La Bourbrille', spreads. Late in spring large, almost upward-facing pink blossoms appear over the blue-green foliage. Next to it, the dwarf broom *Genista decumbens* extends its shoots over the side. This little shrub is covered with golden-yellow blossoms during the spring. The whitish-gray cushion of *Scutella orientalis*—its immediate neighbor—covers the side; it also blooms yellow during late summer. Next to the dwarf juniper and in the background, *Globularia cordifolia* forms dense green dwarf cushions. Squeezed tightly between the rock and the planter edge, *Helichrysum milfordiae* is effective with its silvery white, dense shrubbery. The green mats of Campion, *Silene acaulis* 'Plena', a double-flowering variety of this popular alpine, flows around the rock. Next to it, *Helianthemum canum* spreads over the edge of the planter.

In this planter the ball-shaped dwarf form of *Picea glauca* 'Alberta Globe', supported by several rocks, provides a special accent. In its shade, the autumn-flowering gentian *Gentiana* × *macaulayi* thrives. Along the sunny front, *Silene acaulis* 'Correvoniana' weaves thick mats with reddish pink, double flowers. Between the rocks and dwarf spruce a dwarf Edelweiss, *Leontopodium souliei* 'Mignon', blooms, as does the rosette-forming saxifrage *Saxifraga fritschiana* with white flower panicles and lime-encrusted foliage. The late-blooming White, *Dianthus petraeus* ssp. *noeanus*, forms thick clumps along the edge, and the very dwarf willow, *Salix reticulata*, looks particularly attractive when placed between the rock and the edge where its beautiful foliage is clearly visible.

The interplay of stone and plant in this landscape is especially lively and attractive, due to the many dense, dwarf cushions edging the side of the planter and hugging the rocks.

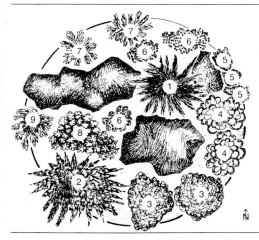

Planter in sunny location. Basic Mix A; diameter 16 in. (40 cm); depth 6 in. (15 cm).

1. *Picea glauca* 'Echiniformis'
2. *Juniperus sabina* 'Skandia'
3. *Helianthemum oelandicum*
4. *Saxifraga paniculata* (syn. *S. aizoon*) 'Balcana'
5. *Vitaliana primuliflora* (syn. *Douglasia vitaliana*) 'Tridentata'
6. *Erinus alpinus* 'Dr. Hähnle'
7. *Edraianthus tenuifolius*
8. *Sempervivella sedoides*
9. *Veronica satureioides* 'Kellereri'

Planter in sunny location. Basic Mix A; diameter 15 in. (38 cm); depth 5½ in. (14 cm).

1. *Juniperus squamata* 'Blue Star', loose-growing
2. *Cytisus decumbens*
3. *Helianthemum canum*
4. *Dianthus* 'La Bourbrille'
5. *Silene acaulis* 'Plena'
6. *Helichrysum milfordiae*
7. *Globularia cordifolia*
8. *Scutellaria orientalis*
9. *Saxifraga callosa* (syn. *S. lingulata*) 'Superba'

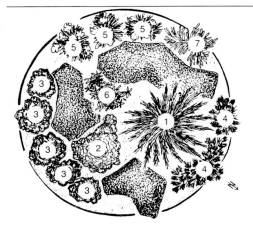

Planter in sunny to partially shaded location. Basic Mix A; diameter 14 in. (35 cm); depth about 5 in. (12 cm).

1. *Picea glauca* 'Alberta Globe'
2. *Saxifraga fritschiana*
3. *Silene acaulis* 'Correvoniana'
4. *Gentiana* × *macaulayi*
5. *Dianthus petraeus* ssp. *noeanus* (syn. *D. noeanus*)
6. *Leontopodium souliei* 'Mignon'
7. *Salix reticulata*

This smaller planter works well due to the sense of quiet which a design with only a few species often creates. A dwarf conifer, *Pinus mugo* 'Mops', as well as several rocks provide special features for this planting. In front of them are the silvery white pillows of *Antennaria dioica* var. *borealis*. On the side are *Arenaria tetraquetra*, with its green mat hard against the rock, and next to the pine a dwarf broom, *Cytisus decumbens*. On the opposite side *Edraianthus graminifolius* provides a blue accent during early spring.

This example proves that even a window box of normal dimensions and made of very ordinary materials can be made into an attractive landscape when planted with hardy dwarf conifers and several flowering rock garden shrubs.

In the center is the slim dwarf False Cypress, *Chamaecyparis lawsoniana* 'Ellwoodii Pygmy', flanked on the left and right by two Japanese dwarf Hinoki Cypresses, *Chamaecyparis obtusa* 'Nana Gracilis'. In the spaces between, two blue creeping junipers, *Juniperus horizontalis* 'Glauca', spread their branches. Between the conifers, the low-growing Oriental Gentian, *Gentiana septemfida* var. *lagodechiana*, blooms during summer, as well as the double-flowered *Petrorhagia saxifraga* 'Plena'.

Window box for sunny locations. Tough, durable planting in Basic Mix A or good topsoil, mixed with sand; length 40 in. (1 m); width 6 in. (15 cm).

Creating an attractive landscape is considerably easier if one has a wider flower box available. For this example, several particularly robust plants were selected. A Filbert cultivar, *Corylus avellana* 'Contorta', provides a special note in this collection. This shrub remains dwarf in a window box. As a counterpoint I selected a dwarf pine, *P. mugo* ssp. *pumilio*. The groundcover is allowed to spread between several rocks. *Veronica incana* forms silvery gray pillows; next to it the red-hued clumps of *Sedum spurium* with their red-flowering form 'Coccineum' spill over the edge. In front is the bluish gray clump of *Dian-thus gratianopolitanus* 'Splendens'. Finally, *Saponaria ocymoides* with its reddish pink, flowering pillow spills over the edge. Behind it is the late-autumn flowering, very dwarf *Aster dumosus* 'Nesthäkchen'; next to a dwarf broom, *Cytisus ardoini*, is the Oriental Gentian, *G. septemfida* 'Erecta'.

Window box for sunny locations; a durable plant collection in Basic Mix A or good topsoil, mixed with sand. Length 40 in. (1 m); width 8 in. (20 cm).

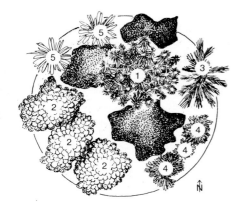

Planter, sunny location. Basic Mix A; diameter 12 in. (30cm); depth 5 in. (12cm).

1. *Pinus mugo* 'Mops'
2. *Antennaria dioica* var. *borealis* (syn. *A. tomentosa* hort.)
3. *Cytisus decumbens*
4. *Arenaria tetraquetra*
5. *Edraianthus graminifolius*

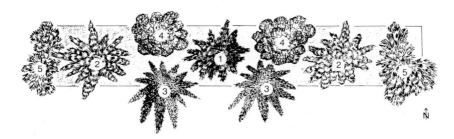

1. *Chamaecyparis lawsoniana* 'Ellwoodii Pygmy'
2. *Chamaecyparis obtusa* 'Nana Gracilis'

3. *Juniperus horizontalis* 'Glauca'
4. *Petrorhagia saxifraga* 'Plena'
5. *Gentiana septemfida* var. *lagodechiana*

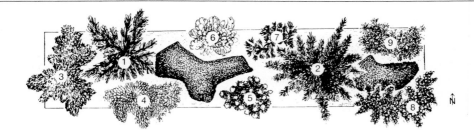

1. *Corylus avellana* 'Contorta'
2. *Pinus mugo* ssp. *pumilio*
3. *Veronica incana*
4. *Sedum spurium* 'Coccineum'

5. *Dianthus gratianopolitanus* 'Splendens'
6. *Cytisus ardoini*
7. *Gentiana septemfida* 'Erecta'
8. *Saponaria ocymoides*
9. *Aster dumosus* 'Nesthäkchen'

139

Even window boxes located in the shade can be attractively landscaped. A striking old root could be used instead of a rock for loosening the design. Next to it the blue-flowering dwarf *Rhododendron impeditum* displays its irregular and loose growth. The counter-balancing focal point is provided by an evergreen dwarf shrub, here *Prunus laurocerasus* 'Otto Luyken'. In the background *Thalictrum dipterocarpum* rises over the other perennials with its airy, purple flower clusters. In front of it is *Campanula poscharskyana* 'Blauranke'; in summer it is loaded with starry blue flowers. On the side *Saxifraga umbrosa* in its yellow-spotted form 'Aureo-Marginata' provides a dense foliage clump. Opposite, another saxifrage, *S. muscoides* 'Findling', displays its delicate foliage, and behind it the winter-flowering *Erica herbacea* 'Winter Beauty.'

This window box was planted exclusively with alpine plants. Between several rocks an elegant *Pinus parviflora* 'Glauca' rises, and in such a container it will never grow too large. Across from it a dwarf spruce, *Picea glauca* 'Echiniformis', was planted for contrast and another focal point. The third focus is the outstanding *Euryops evansii*, a dwarf shrub with silvery foliage and golden blossoms during summer. Edge plants are the red rosettes of *Sempervivum* 'Rubin'; in front of the green, a dwarf clump of Campion, *Silene acaulis*, bears the reddish, double blooms of the cultivar 'Correvoniana'. Next to it, the smallest of the brooms, *Genista villarsii*, extends its branches over the edge. Enclosed by several rocks, the rosette pillows of *Saxifraga paniculata* are joined. In the background, between rock and edge, is *Draba bruniifolia* var. *diversifolia*. The white pendulous blooms of *Minuartia laricifolia* drape over the edge of the window box, and its neighbor, *Androsace sempervivoides*, forms dense clumps. In the background *Primula auricula*, the primrose of the Alps, appears very decoratively dressed in large, dusted leaves. Right next to it *Chrysanthemum weyrichii* spreads its green foliage clump.

This is an 8-in.-wide (20 cm) window box with alpine plants surrounding perforated limestone rocks. Especially interesting here is a very narrow, stiff, columnar pine, *Pinus sylvestris* 'Fastigiata', and in contrast, the low globular *Pinus sylvestris* 'Perkeo'. *Dryas octopetala* drapes over the side. The corners are marked by *Acantholimon glumaceum* and *Onosma albo-rosea*. Between them: *Saxifraga callosa* 'Bellardi', *Draba lasiocarpa*, *Saxifraga paniculata* 'Minutifolia' and *Arenaria arduinii*—a beautiful border of stiff rosettes and various forms of dwarf foliage. Between the rocks *Androsace sarmentosa* 'Watkinsii' provides its beautiful, gray, woolly clumps. At the rear is *Aethionema grandiflorum*, *Minuartia subnivalis*, *Daphne rosetti*, in the middle another *Aethionema*, and finally the white-leaved *Andryala agardhii*.

Window box for a sunny location: alpine plants. Basic Mix B or A amended with sand; length 40 in. (1 m); width 8 in. (20 cm).

1. *Pinus sylvestris* 'Fastigiata'
2. *Pinus sylvestris* 'Perkeo'

140

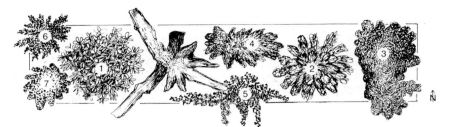

Window box for shady areas. Basic Mix A; length 40 in. (1 m); width 8 in. (20 cm).

1. *Rhododendron impeditum*
2. *Prunus laurocerasus* 'Otto Luyken'
3. *Saxifraga umbrosa* 'Aureo-Marginata'
4. *Thalictrum dipterocarpum*
5. *Campanula poscharskyana* 'Blauranke'
6. *Erica herbacea* 'Winter Beauty'
7. *Saxifraga muscoides* 'Findling'

Window box for sunny locations planted with alpine plants in Basic Mix A. Length 32 in. (80 cm); width 6 in. (15 cm).

1. *Pinus parviflora* 'Glauca'
2. *Picea glauca* 'Echiniformis'
3. *Euryops evansii*
4. *Sempervivum* 'Rubin'
5. *Draba bruniifolia* var. *diversifolia*
6. *Genista villarsii*
7. *Silene acaulis* 'Correvoniana'
8. *Saxifraga paniculata*
9. *Chrysanthemum weyrichii*
10. *Minuartia laricifolia*
11. *Primula auricula*
12. *Androsace sempervivoides*

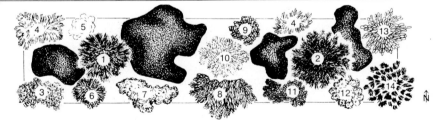

3. *Acantholimon glumaceum*
4. *Aethionema grandiflorum*
5. *Minuartia subnivalis*
6. *Saxifraga callosa* 'Bellardi'
7. *Draba lasiocarpa*
8. *Dryas octopetala*
9. *Daphne rosetti*
10. *Androsace sarmentosa* 'Watkinsii'
11. *Saxifraga paniculata* 'Minutifolia'
12. *Arenaria arduinii*
13. *Andryala agardhii*
14. *Onosma albo-rosea*

Too often it is thought that only *Sedum* or *Sempervivum* species can be successfully grown in low, shallow troughs. In truth, there is a sufficient selection among alpine plants to provide for a marvelously varied planting in a shallow trough.

The landscape in this 6 in. (15 cm) deep splash slab is characterized by only a slight increase in height by virtue of the rocks. On the slope's edge, a dwarf pine, *Pinus sylvestris* 'Perkeo', is planted. In the background, between the large rosettes of *Saxifraga cotyledon* the loose flowers of *Petrorhagia saxifraga* 'Plena' bloom almost all summer long. Low-growing *Iberis saxatilis* drapes its foliage over the side of the trough. *Saponaria caespitosa* borders the front edge with its solid, green clumps. Its pink blossoms sit at the end of 3–4 in. (7–10 cm) stems. On the opposite corner, *Dianthus simulans* covers the trough with dense foliage. The stiff, dwarf foliage of *Gypsophila tenuifolia* mediates between them. Among the rocks the rosette mats of *Sempervivum* 'Beta' and 'Rubin' spread. The latter cultivar produces bright garnet rosettes; between them, the light, silvery gray pillows of *Sedum spathulifolium* 'Cape Blanco' make an especially attractive contrast.

The basic structure for this landscape is created by the dense, globe-shaped, dwarf Japanese *Cryptomeria japonica* 'Vilmoriniana', the blue-needled *Picea glauca* 'Echiniformis' and —spreading over the edge—*Picea abies* 'Inversa', a trailing spruce that can be kept dwarf constrained in a trough. Around this structure, the planting concentrates on *Saxifraga* species. Especially obvious is the single rosette of *S. longifolia*. Between the rocks, *S. oppositifolia* develops a low cushion. Several early-flowering saxifrages of the Kabschia group complete the planting: *S. grisebachii* 'Wisley'; *S. borisii*, with ashen-colored, dense foliage; as well as *S. sancta*, with fresh green leaves. *Sempervivella sedoides* offers a very pretty foliage structure with creamy flowers, and thrives in either sunny or shady sites. Next to it are the decorative leaves of *Primula marginata*, a rock primrose. The corner is taken over by the long-blooming *Cymbalaria muralis* 'Globosa Rosea'. *Thlaspi rotundifolium* creates dwarf cushions between the rocks and the edge of the trough. *Ramonda myconi* and *Gentiana* × *macaulayi*, an autumn-flowering gentian, finish the design.

This example illustrates how low troughs can be planted attractively. A commercially produced planter made of fiber glass and mortar is placed in a shaded location and then planted with the purplish-flowering *Rhododendron impeditum*, a Himalayan native. Particularly note that it is a looser-structured form in contrast to the more common dense, twiggy form. In front *Juniperus horizontalis* 'Glauca' grows over the edge, framed by a *Campanula portenschlagiana* 'Birch Hybrid' and *Ramonda myconi*. Between several rocks are the large rosettes of *Saxifraga cotyledon* 'Southside Seedling'. This new hybrid has gorgeous, much-divided panicles with reddish white, single flowers. Next to the dark green leaves of *Primula clusiana*, a Rock Primrose with purple flowers, *Soldanella montana*, thrives. Unfortunately, this plant usually flowers very sparsely, but when its fringed, violet flowers appear early in spring, what a beautiful sight! Next to the golden yellow-flowering Alpine Primrose, *Primula auricula*, is *Wulfenia carinthiaca*. In summer, blue flower clusters emerge from its shiny green foliage.

Trough for sunny sites; Basic Mix A. Length 24 in. (60 cm); width 22 in. (55 cm); depth 6 in. (15 cm).

1. *Pinus sylvestris* 'Perkeo'
2. *Saxifraga cotyledon*
3. *Petrorhagia saxifraga* (syn. *Tunica saxifraga*) 'Plena'
4. *Iberis saxatilis*
5. *Saponaria caespitosa*
6. *Sempervivum* 'Beta'
7. *Sedum spathulifolium* 'Cape Blanco'
8. *Sempervivum* 'Beta'
9. *Gypsophila tenuifolia*
10. *Dianthus simulans*

1. *Picea abies* 'Inversa'
2. *Cryptomeria japonica* 'Vilmoriniana'
3. *Picea glauca* 'Echiniformis'
4. *Sempervivella sedoides*
5. *Saxifraga longifolia*
6. *Thlaspi rotundifolium*
7. *Ramonda myconi*
8. *Saxifraga borisii*
9. *Saxifraga oppositifolia*
10. *Gentiana* × *macaulayi*
11. *Saxifraga grisebachii* 'Wisley'
12. *Cymbalaria muralis* (syn. *Linaria cymbalaria*) 'Globosa Rosea'
13. *Saxifraga sancta*
14. *Primula marginata*

Trough for a shaded site. Basic Mix A; length 40 in. (1 m); width 20 in. (50 cm); depth 13½ in. (34 cm).

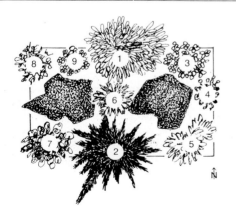

Trough made of a composite material for a shaded site. Basic Mix D or A amended with peat moss; length 24 in. (60 cm); width 14 in. (36 cm); depth 6 in. (15 cm).

1. *Rhododendron impeditum*
2. *Juniperus horizontalis* 'Glauca'
3. *Primula clusiana*
4. *Soldanella montana*
5. *Ramonda myconi*
6. *Saxifraga cotyledon* 'Southside Seedling'
7. *Campanula portenschlagiana* 'Birch Hybrid'
8. *Wulfenia carinthiaca*
9. *Primula auricula*

143

This homemade trough is of ideal dimensions. Setting the tone is a dwarf Blue Pine, *P. pumila* 'Glauca', located next to several rocks; its growth habit is reminiscent of a Japanese bonsai. The tree should not be so small that it cannot provide an attractive focal point as soon as planted. Its companion piece, *Picea glauca* 'Laurin', is completely symmetrical, dense, and of a conical habit. This dwarf spruce must be at least 10–20 years old in order to provide an effective balance; it is very slow-growing. Between these poles the low-growing, dense globe of *Picea mariana* 'Nana' provides another relationship with its bluish gray foliage. The picturesque trailing edge planting consists of Blue Juniper, *J. horizontalis* 'Glauca', a dwarf willow, *Salix* × *simulatrix*, the American *Dryas drummondii* and *Dianthus petraeus* ssp. *noeanus*. Next to a silver-webbed *Sempervivum* 'Shootrolds Triumph', the narrow-leaved rosettes of *Saxifraga callosa* 'Superba' spread between the rocks. In the dense shade of rock and dwarf pine, *Primula clusiana* and *Campanula poscharskyana* 'Blauranke' will thrive. *Saxifraga trifurcata* bears white blooms for weeks; late in the year, the purplish red flowers of *Aster dumosus* 'Nesthäkchen' complete the flowering season.

In this old stone trough, several interesting-looking rocks are absolutely essential. A dwarf spruce, *Picea glauca* 'Laurin', and a dwarf broom, *Genista villarsii*, define the design; the latter will descend down the side of the trough. In one corner is *Leontopodium souliei*, an easy-to-grow Edelweiss from the Himalayas. The other corner is occupied by a rosette of *Saxifraga cotyledon*. The grasslike, green, dwarf foliage of *Gypsophila tenuifolia* hugs the rocks alongside the reddish brown rosettes of *Sempervivum blandum*. Next to green, dwarf, clumps of *Saponaria* × *oliviana*, the grayish blue cushions of *Dianthus sylvestris* trail over the front. Planted along the left side, *Minuartia laricifolia* flowers in late spring with white blossoms covering the trailing foliage; this is bordered by a clump of tiny rosettes of *Saxifraga paniculata* 'Baldensis'. The planting of this trough highlights the effect of the rock formations especially well. Strictly low-growing, dense foliage hugs the rock that is surmounted only by the dwarf spruce.

Several rocks and a background planting of the dwarf *Picea abies* 'Echiniformis' set the alpine tone of this trough. Next to the dwarf spruce, *Veronica armena* 'Rosea' builds a loose clump. In front of it and somewhat elevated between the rocks, a true Edelweiss, *Leontopodium alpinum vera*, thrives and presents well-formed, silvery white blossoms. The flower is supported by silvery gray foliage, and the white bloom is accented by a dwarf *Scleranthus uniflorus* with its distinctive brown foliage. This plant really enjoys a location in a narrow crevice. *Armeria juniperifolia* also forms dense dwarf clumps. In front of it in the corner of the trough, *Arenaria ledebouriana* is covered during the blooming period in late spring with fragrant, loosely structured flower clumps. The silver-colored foliage pillows of *Artemisia umbelliformis* occupy the front of the trough next to the green cushion of *Silene acaulis*, here the reddish pink-flowering dwarf form 'Excapa'. Early in spring the Kabschia saxifrage *S. sancta* completes the alpine image with its grayish green foliage. *Minuartia parnassica* orients itself with dense, stiff leaves between rock and at the edge of the trough. This planting depends especially heavily on the selection of rocks to provide the trough with the appropriate impact.

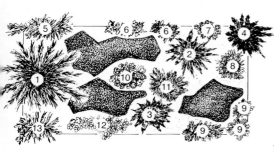

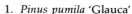

1. *Pinus pumila* 'Glauca'
2. *Picea glauca* 'Laurin'
3. *Picea mariana* 'Nana'
4. *Juniperus horizontalis* 'Glauca'
5. *Salix* × *simulatrix*
6. *Dryas drummondii*
7. *Dianthus petraeus* ssp. *noeanus* (syn. *D. noeanus*)
8. *Aster dumosus* 'Nesthäkchen'
9. *Saxifraga trifurcata*
10. *Sempervivum* 'Shootrolds Triumph'
11. *Saxifraga callosa* (syn. *S. lingulata*) 'Superba'
12. *Primula clusiana*
13. *Campanula poscharskyana* 'Blauranke'

Trough for sunny site. Basic Mix A; length 40 in. (1 m); width 20 in. (50 cm); depth 12 in. (30 cm).

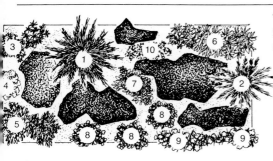

Trough for a sunny site. Basic Mix A; length 32 in. (80 cm); width 16 in. (40 cm); depth 10 in. (26 cm).

1. *Picea glauca* 'Laurin'
2. *Genista villarsii*
3. *Leontopodium souliei*
4. *Minuartia laricifolia*
5. *Saxifraga paniculata* (syn. *S. aizoon*) 'Baldensis'
6. *Saxifraga cotyledon*
7. *Sempervivum blandum*
8. *Saponaria* × *oliviana*
9. *Dianthus sylvestris*
10. *Gypsophila tenuifolia*

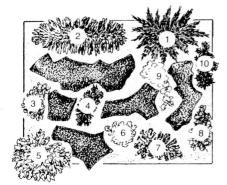

Trough for a sunny site. Basic Mix A; length 24 in. (62 cm); width 19 in. (48 cm); depth 12 in. (30 cm).

1. *Picea abies* 'Echiniformis'
2. *Veronica armena* 'Rosea'
3. *Armeria juniperifolia* (syn. *A. caespitosa*)
4. *Leontopodium alpinum vera*
5. *Arenaria ledebouriana*
6. *Artemisia umbelliformis* (syn. *A. laxa*)
7. *Silene acaulis* 'Excapa'
8. *Minuartia parnassica*
9. *Scleranthus uniflorus*
10. *Saxifraga sancta*

Construction and planting of this sun-loving trough is depicted in color plates (1–6). Here several dwarf conifers together with perforated limestone boulders dominate the scene. The dwarf spruce, *Picea glauca* 'Echiniformis', creates the background; in the foreground *Juniperus horizontalis* 'Glauca' grows over the trough's edge. Also in front is a clump of *Phlox douglasii* 'Eva', bordered toward the center of the trough by a rock. Next to this is the spring-flowering gentian, *G. acaulis* 'Dinarica', as well as the reddish brown *Sempervivum* 'Rubin'. The silver-webbed rosettes of *Sempervivum arachnoideum* ssp. *tomentosum* reside in the holes of the perforated rock. Squeezed in the cracks between the rocks is the large rosette of *Saxifraga longifolia*. Behind the rocks an Edelweiss, *Leontopodium alpinum*, peers from one side of the trough. On the other side, *Erinus alpinus* 'Dr. Hähnle' provides a splash of welcome color with its carmine-red spring flowers. Almost hidden by the creeping juniper, limited from spreading inward by a strategically placed rock, *Anthyllis webbiana* flourishes. Early in summer its violet flowers appear over green foliage cushions.

In Basic Mix D, a low-growing *Rhododendron keleticum* from the Himalayas thrives along the trough's edge. In the background is the large, red-flowering Japanese Azalea 'Muttertag'; somewhat at a distance is the dwarf, dark pink-salmon *Rhododendron multiflorum* 'Alpengarten'. In the foreground is the Bellflower, *Campanula portenschlagiana* 'Birch Hybrid' and *Minuartia laricifolia*. The latter plant, which properly belongs in a sunny spot in Basic Mix A, indicates how adaptable some of the alpine plants can be. Between perforated limestone and also out of its holes the silvery gray foliage rosettes of *Saxifraga cotyledon* 'Pyramidalis' emerge in considerable size. On the north side *Saxifraga* × *apiculata* and *Saxifraga sancta* form dense, green, dwarf clumps. At the edge *Ramonda myconi* creates beautiful, somewhat hairy, leaf rosettes.

In the section filled with Basic Mix A, the ball-shaped dwarf spruce, *Picea glauca* 'Echiniformis', and a dwarf Balsam Fir, *Abies balsamea* 'Nana', define the design. Over the trough edge, the summer blossoms of *Gentiana septemfida* var. *lagodechiana* and the dense, grayish blue clumps of *Dianthus gratianopolitanus* 'Compactus' drape their treasures. In the background the Alpine Primrose, *Primula auricula*, displays its lightly dusted, large foliage which is of great ornamental value even without benefit of the yellow, spring flowers. Between these *Campanula cochleariifolia* spreads—often all too easily! The finish is provided by the rosettes of *Saxifraga callosa* 'Lantoscana' with pure white flower panicles early in summer. This trough has plants blooming from spring well into autumn.

146

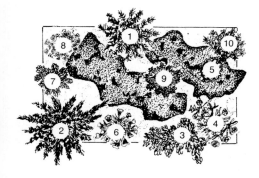

Trough for a sunny location. Basic Mix A; length 23 in. (60 cm); width 15 in. (38 cm); depth 10 in. (26 cm).

1. *Picea glauca* 'Echiniformis'
2. *Juniperus horizontalis* 'Glauca'
3. *Phlox douglasii* 'Eva'
4. *Sempervivum* 'Rubin'
5. *Sempervivum arachnoideum* ssp. *tomentosum*
6. *Gentiana acaulis* 'Dinarica'
7. *Anthyllis webbiana*
8. *Erinus alpinus* 'Dr. Hähnle'
9. *Saxifraga longifolia*
10. *Leontopodium alpinum*

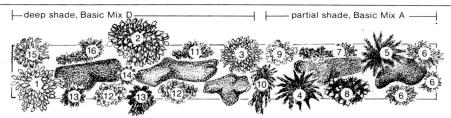

Trough in partial to deep shade. Half-filled with Basic Mix A, the shady portion filled with Basic Mix D; length 9 ft. (275 cm); width 18 in. (45 cm); depth 10 in. (25 cm).

1. *Rhododendron keleticum*
2. Japanese *Azalea* 'Muttertag'
3. *Rhododendron multiflorum* 'Alpengarten'
4. *Picea glauca* 'Echiniformis'
5. *Abies balsamea* 'Nana'
6. *Saxifraga callosa* (syn. *S. lingulata*) 'Lantoscana'
7. *Campanula cochleariifolia* (syn. *C. pusilla*)
8. *Dianthus gratianopolitanus* (syn. *D. caesus*) 'Compactus'
9. *Primula auricula*
10. *Gentiana septemfida* var. *lagodechiana*
11. *Saxifraga* × *apiculata*
12. *Campanula portenschlagiana* 'Birch Hybrid'
13. *Minuartia laricifolia*
14. *Saxifraga cotyledon* 'Pyramidalis'
15. *Ramonda myconi*
16. *Saxifraga sancta*

Appendix: Societies

Alpine Garden Society
   The Secretary, Lye End Link, St. John's
   Woking, Surrey GU21 1SW, United
   Kingdom.
American Rock Garden Society
   The Secretary, 15 Fairmead Road,
   Darien, Connecticut 06820, U.S.A.
New Zealand Alpine Garden Society
   The Secretary, 17 Courage Road,
   Amberley, New Zealand.
Scottish Rock Garden Club
   The Secretary, 21 Erchiston Park, Edin-
   burgh EH10 4PW, United Kingdom.
Vancouver Island Rock and Alpine
   Garden Society
   The Secretary, P. O. Box 6507, Station
   C, Victoria, B.C. V8P 5M4, Canada.

Selected Bibliography

Journals

Alpine Garden Society. *Alpine Gardening* 1986–.

Alpine Garden Society. *Quarterly Bulletin.* 1930–.

American Rock Garden Society. *Bulletin.* 1942–.

Books

Alpines '86 Publications Committee. *Rocky Mountain Alpines*. Timber Press Inc., 1986.

Bacon, L. *Mountain Flower Holidays in Europe*. Alpine Garden Society, 1979.

Bawden, H. E. *Dwarf Shrubs*. Alpine Garden Society, 1980.

Brickell, C. D. & Matthew, B. *Daphne*. Alpine Garden Society, 1976.

Coombes, A. J. *Dictionary of Plant Names*. Timber Press, Inc. and Collingridge, 1987.

Cribb, P. & Butterfield, I. *The Genus Pleione*. Timber Press, Inc. and Christopher Helm Publishers Ltd., 1988.

Dryden, E. *Alpines in Pots*. Alpine Garden Society, 1988.

Elliott, J. *Alpines in Sinks and Troughs*. Alpine Garden Society, 1975.

Elliott, R. *Alpine Gardening*. Alpine Garden Society, reprinted 1988.

Foster, H. L. & L. L. *Rock Gardening*. Timber Press, Inc., 1968.

Good, J. *Handbook of Rock Gardening*. Alpine Garden Society, 1988.

Grey-Wilson, C. *Dionysia*. Alpine Garden Society, 1989.

Grey-Wilson, C. *The Genus Cyclamen*. Timber Press, Inc. and Christopher Helm Publishers Ltd., 1988.

Grey-Wilson, C. editor. *A Manual of Alpine and Rock Garden Plants*. Timber Press, Inc. and Christopher Helm Publishers Ltd., 1989.

Harkness, M. G. & D'Angelo, D. *The Bernard Harkness Seedlist Handbook*. Timber Press, Inc., 1986.

Hulme, J. K. *Propagation of Alpine Plants*. Alpine Garden Society, 1982.

Ingwersen, W. *Manual of Alpine Plants*. Timber Press, Inc. and Collingridge, 1986.

Köhlein, F. *Saxifrages and Related Genera*. Timber Press, Inc., 1984.

Mathew, B. *The Crocus*. Timber Press, Inc. and B. T. Batsford Ltd., 1982.

Mathew, B. *The Iris*. Timber Press, Inc. and B. T. Batsford Ltd., revised edition, 1989.

Mathew, B. *The Smaller Bulbs*. B. T. Batsford Ltd., 1987.

Plant Finder. Hardy Plant Society/Headmain, annually.

Polunin, O. *Flowers of Greece and the Balkans*. Oxford U. P., 1980.

Polunin, O. & Stainton, A. *Flowers of the Himalaya*. Oxford U. P., 1984.

Smith, G. F. & Lowe, D. *Androsace*. Alpine Garden Society, 1977.

Smith, G. F. *et al*. *Primulas of Europe and America*. Alpine Garden Society, 1984.

Webb, D. A. & Gornall, R. J. *A Manual of Saxifrages*. Timber Press, Inc. and Christopher Helm Publishers Ltd., 1989.

Yeo, P. *Hardy Geraniums*. Timber Press, Inc. and Christopher Helm Publishers Ltd., 1985.

Index to Common Names

Page numbers in italics note illustrations.

Index to Botanical Names

Page numbers in italics note illustrations.

Illustration Credits

Color photos 1–6, 26, 59, 62, 67–68 by
 Flora-bild (A. Felbinger).
Color photos 7, 13, 15, 16, 18, 23, 69, 70 by
 Franz Stöhr, Rutesheim.
All other photos by the author.
Garden plans by Regina Brendel,
 Pfungstadt.
All other line drawings by Emil Wetter,
 Rutesheim.